ASSESSING THE CAREER OF HISTORIAN
THOMAS G. ALEXANDER

Charles Redd Monographs in Western History

ASSESSING THE CAREER OF HISTORIAN
THOMAS G. ALEXANDER

JAY H. BUCKLEY, EDITOR

Assessing the Career of Historian Thomas G. Alexander

The Charles Redd Monographs in Western History are made possible by the generous contributions of Charles and Annaley Naegle Redd and their family. Their donations served as the basis for the establishment of the Charles Redd Center for Western Studies at Brigham Young University in 1972. The Redd Center remains one of the oldest and most important centers focused on supporting western studies in the American and Intermountain West.

Copyright © 2024 by the BYU Charles Redd Center for Western Studies

Published by the BYU Charles Redd Center for Western Studies

Redd Center director and editor: Jay H. Buckley
Copy editing, cover design, and interior formatting: Amy M. Carlin

Punctuation and capitalization in quotations may be modernized or altered for clarity.

Ordering Information:
IngramSpark at www.ingramspark.com or
Amazon-Books at www.amazon.com
Or through your local bookstore

No part of this publication may be used or reproduced in any manner whatsoever without written permission, except in the case of brief quotations embodied in critical articles, or reviews, or for teaching purposes.

Requests for reproduction or other permission should be addressed to the Charles Redd Center for Western Studies at redd_center@byu.edu

Redd Center website: reddcenter.byu.edu

Printed in the United States of America, International, by permission

ISBN: 978-0-9986960-5-8

ALL RIGHTS RESERVED

CONTENTS

Prologue — 1
    Jay H. Buckley, Director, Charles Redd Center for Western Studies, Brigham Young University

Preface — 5
    Richard W. Etulain, Professor Emeritus of History, University of New Mexico

Thomas G. Alexander: Distinguished Scholar of Mormon and Utah History — 8
    Barbara Jones Brown, Director, Signature Books Publishing

Thomas G. Alexander: Environmental Stewardship in the American West — 17
    Sara Dant, Brady Presidential Distinguished Professor and Chair of History, Weber State University

Thomas G. Alexander: Native American History and Future Scholarship — 24
    Farina Noelani King (Diné), Associate Professor of Native American Studies, University of Oklahoma

Reply to Comments at the 2021 Western History Association Conference, Portland, Oregon — 32
    Thomas G. Alexander, Lemuel Hardison Redd Jr. Professor Emeritus of Western American History at Brigham Young University

Epilogue: Brief Biography of Thomas Glen Alexander — 41
    Jay H. Buckley, Director, Charles Redd Center for Western Studies, Brigham Young University

Curriculum Vitae of Thomas G. Alexander — 44
    Revised March 2024

PROLOGUE

Jay H. Buckley, Director, Charles Redd Center for Western Studies, Brigham Young University

On October 28, 2021, I sat in a well-attended session of the Western History Association in Portland, Oregon, entitled "Assessing the Career of Historian Thomas G. Alexander." I had just finished writing the final draft of *A Golden Jubilee History: The Charles Redd Center for Western Studies at Brigham Young University, 1972–2022*, which was subsequently published in March of 2022. The center's history was fresh on my mind: Historian Leonard J. Arrington had been appointed as both the center's first director in January 1972 and the Lemuel Hardison Redd Jr. Professor of Western American History, an endowed chair in the history department at Brigham Young University. At the same time, he was called as Church historian for The Church of Jesus Christ of Latter-day Saints, so the Church and the university arranged for Arrington to work half time at each establishment.

With the consent of history department chair Ted Warner, Leonard asked Thomas G. Alexander to serve as associate director of the center. Leonard and Tom had worked together while Tom was a master's student at Utah State University and while Tom completed his doctoral work at the University of California at Berkeley. Together they coauthored a series of articles on Utah's defense installations. In 1980, Leonard was released as church historian, resigned as Redd Center director, and assumed the directorship of the Joseph Fielding Smith Institute for Church History at BYU. Tom was appointed to fill the vacancy as Redd Center director, a position he held for the next twelve years, marking

2021 Western History Association panel consisting of Barbara Jones Brown, Farina Noelani King, Richard W. Etulain, Thomas G. Alexander, Sara Dant. Photo courtesy of Jay H. Buckley.

two decades as director or associate director at the center during its formative years. In 1992, Tom was appointed Lemuel Hardison Redd Jr. Professor of Western American History, an endowed chair that he held until his retirement from the university in 2004.

Since the center's creation on January 20, 1972, made possible by the generous contributions of Charles and Annaley Naegle Redd, the Redd Center remains one of the oldest and most important interdiscilpinary centers focused on supporting western studies in the American and Intermountain West and Thomas G. Alexander has been affiliated with it since its inception. He remains a valuable and active member of the Redd Center board of directors at age 89.

It was altogether fitting that approximately fifty years after the Redd Center's creation, friends and colleagues gathered to reflect upon the remarkable career of this distinguished historian and superb gentleman. Tom's longtime friend, prolific author and prize-winning historian Richard W. Etulain, Professor Emeritus of History at the University of New Mexico, chaired the session and introduced the participants and their topics.

Barbara Jones Brown was first to present. She is the former executive director of the Mormon History Association, former historical director of Better Days 2020, and content editor of *Massacre at Mountain Meadows* (2008). She currently serves as director of Signature Books Publishing and recently co-authored the award-winning *Vengeance Is Mine: The Mountain Meadows Massacre and Its Aftermath* (2023). She was ideally positioned to present "Thomas G. Alexander: Distinguished Scholar of Mormon and Utah History," discussing his contributions in these fields.

We then had the pleasure to hear from Sara Dant, Brady Presidential Distinguished Professor and Chair of History at Weber State University. Dant is a prize-winning author of articles and books on environmental history. Her latest book is a completely revised and updated edition of *Losing Eden: An Environmental History of the American West* (2023). She presented on "Thomas Alexander and Environmental Stewardship in the American West."

The third presenter was Farina Noelani King (*Diné*), then affiliated with Northeastern State University, now the Horizon Chair of Native Ecology and Culture and associate professor of Native American studies at the University of Oklahoma. Author of the award-winning *The Earth Memory Compass: Diné Landscapes and Education in the Twentieth Century* (2018), co-author of *Returning Home: Diné Creative Works from the Intermountain Indian School* (2021), and author of *Gáamalii dóó Diné: Navajo Latter-day Saint Experiences in the Twentieth Century* (2023), King focused her remarks on "Thomas Alexander and Native American History and Future Scholarship."

Tom then read his own prepared, written comments.

In the months that followed, I asked each of them if they would be willing to consider publishing their essays in a small Redd Center monograph series, and they graciously consented. I encouraged them to maintain the informal style they had used in the session with their dear friend and colleague Tom, with the addition of references.

Arrington and Alexander had started publishing the Charles Redd Monographs in Western History series in 1972. These slender gray volumes featured shorter publications between the length of scholarly articles and academic monographs. Alexander served as an editor or contributor to each of the first eight monographs published by the Redd Center. It is entirely fitting and appropriate to have this edited volume published in the same series. I extend my sincerest thanks to Barbara, Farina, Sara, and Tom for consenting to have their essays published and to Dick for kindly writing the preface.

I express my sincere gratitude to Redd Center Office Supervisor Amy M. Carlin, who completed the final editing and layout for this publication. I thank Charlie and Annaley Redd for establishing the Redd Center and their family's continued support through the Redd Foundation. The Redd, Butler, Peters, Embry, Dixon–Taylor, and Walker families have contributed greatly to the center and their efforts have advanced western studies throughout the Intermountain West.

PREFACE

Richard W. Etulain, Professor Emeritus of History, University of New Mexico

When I heard about a special session to honor Thomas G. Alexander at the Western History Association (WHA) in Portland, Oregon, I was delighted to be involved in its planning. During this well-attended session "Assessing the Career of Historian Thomas Alexander" on October 28, 2021, we enjoyed hearing the following presentations:

> *Session Chair*: Richard W. Etulain, University of New Mexico (Emeritus)
> "Thomas Alexander: Distinguished Historian of Utah," by Barbara Jones Brown, Mormon History Association
> "Thomas Alexander and Environmental Stewardship in the American West." by Sara Dant, Weber State University
> "Thomas Alexander and Native American History and Future Scholarship," by Farina King (Dine'), Northeastern State University [now, University of Oklahoma].
> "Comment," by Thomas Glen Alexander, Brigham Young University

It was a pleasure and a privilege to chair the session and introduce my colleague and long-time friend Tom Alexander. We have been attending WHA conferences together for about a half century, I have read his books for nearly that long, and—well—we've been western historians and men of faith together for a long time. Tom is the Lemuel Hardison Redd Jr. Professor Emeritus of Western American History at Brigham Young University. For more than a half century, he has been a notable teacher of western history, Mormon history, Utah history, and environmental history, teaching thousands of students.

In addition, Tom has been a notably prolific publisher, authoring or editing thirty books and more than 150 essays. From his first book, *A Clash of Interests* (1977), to his most recent volume, *Brigham Young and the Expansion of the Mormon Faith* (2019), Tom has displayed his wide interests in diverse subjects. His award-winning books include *Things of Heaven and Earth* (1991) and *Utah: The Right Place* (3rd ed. 2012). His valuable writings and teaching have won prizes including the Evans Biography Award, Daughters of the American Revolution History Award, and BYU's Distinguished Faculty Leadership Award.

Tom has been a leader in several organizations. He served as president of the Pacific Coast Branch of the American History Association, Phi Alpha Theta, and the Mormon History Association. He has also made major contributions to the WHA, serving on several major committees and as WHA parliamentarian for nearly forty years.

Tom is likewise a strong churchman and devoted husband and father. He is married to Marilyn Johns Alexander, and they are the parents of five children and grandparents of six grandchildren.

Finally, because of all these strong and notable performances as prize-winning teacher and prolific publisher, Tom inherited the mantle as the foremost Latter-day Saint historian from Leaonard Arrington. The mantle remains with him in every way.

—Dick Etulain

THOMAS G. ALEXANDER: DISTINGUISHED SCHOLAR OF MORMON AND UTAH HISTORY

Barbara Jones Brown, Director, Signature Books Publishing

Assessing the Career of Historian Thomas G. Alexander

No historian has contributed more to the scholarship and understanding of Mormon and Utah history than Thomas G. Alexander. His prolific publications include thirty books and monographs and 150 articles—most of them on Utah history and many of them prize-winning works. Religious studies historian Jan Shipps has said that Tom is probably the only Mormon historian whose work she has not read in its entirety because he is so prolific.[1]

During his forty years as faculty in the history department at Brigham Young University, he taught Utah history, Mormon history, Western history, and environmental history to thousands of students. Many of them have gone on to become influential scholars of Utah and Mormon history themselves, including university professors, directors at the Charles Redd Center for Western Studies, managing directors of Salt Lake City's Church History Library, and editors of the *Utah Historical Quarterly, the Journal of Mormon History*, and the BYU Press.[2]

Tom's service in the humanities is exceptional. He has served as chair or president of the Utah Board of State History; the Utah Humanities Council; the Association of Utah Historians; the Mormon History Association; the Western History Association; the Sons of the Utah Pioneers; the Utah Valley Historical Society; the Provo City Landmarks Commission; the Utah Academy of Sciences, Arts, and Letters; the Pacific Coast Branch of the American Historical Association; and the national history honor society, Phi Alpha Theta.[3]

Tom's upbringing and education shaped his desire to become a scholar of Utah and Mormon history. Born in the northern Utah town of Logan and raised not far south of there in the city of Ogden, young Tom developed an interest in social studies. He began his college education at Ogden's Weber State University with a scholarship in that field. Tom's engineer father, however, had other ideas for his son, urging him to go into his own field. For a time, Tom put his interest in social studies on hold, earning an associate degree in mechanical engineering at Weber State and then completing another quarter in that major at Salt Lake City's University of Utah. The world might never have known the historian Tom Alexander had he not then been called to serve in the West German Mission for The Church of Jesus Christ of Latter-day Saints from 1956 to 1958. Those two years far from home gave him the space to realize he really did not want to be an engineer.[4]

After returning home, Tom transferred to Logan's Utah State University to study under noted historians George Ellsworth and Leonard Arrington. There he earned his bachelor's and master's degrees in political science and history. Tom considered Ellsworth the best teacher he ever had, as well as an excellent writer and wordsmith who helped him develop his own teaching and writing skills. From Arrington, Tom learned how to be productive in research and writing, or "how to get things done," as Tom put it.

After Tom went on to UC Berkeley to earn a PhD, he and Arrington collaborated on a series of articles on military defense installations in Utah. "Essentially, I would do the research and write a draft," Tom explained, and then Leonard "would work through the article." These articles were published in the *Utah Historical Quarterly* and the *Pacific Historical Review* while Tom was still in graduate school.[5]

At Arrington's suggestion, Tom wrote his doctoral dissertation on the financial relationship between the US Department of the Interior and the Intermountain Territories from 1863, when Idaho and Arizona territories were organized, to 1896, when Utah became a state.

Tom completed his PhD in American history in 1965—a good time to graduate, as higher education was expanding in the 1960s and a large number of positions were available in history. At this point, Tom came to another crossroads in his career path. Fresno State University offered him a position, wanting him to become its specialist in California history. Simultaneously, Brigham Young University also made him an offer. Tom decided he was more interested in Western history, particularly Utah and Mormon history, and so he accepted the offer from BYU.[6]

He served on the BYU faculty for forty years, teaching Western, Utah, and Mormon history classes. He also created BYU's first environmental history course. Tom was grateful for the strong funding he had at BYU. "I had all the money I needed to do the things I needed to do—for research, going to historical conferences and so forth," he said.

That funding made possible his decades of affiliation with the Western History Association (WHA). During his first year on BYU's faculty, Tom and fellow history faculty members Jim Allen and Ted Warner piled into Jim's old station wagon and drove to the 1964 conference in Oklahoma. "Ted and I were a bit embarrassed to ride with Jim, who had a 'Goldwater for President' sticker on the back of his car," Tom remembered. But the three had a great experience at WHA, and "we traveled a great deal to history conventions together after that." Within a few years, Tom began serving as parliamentarian of WHA.[7]

Tom eventually published his doctoral dissertation as a book titled, *A Clash of Interests: Interior Department and Mountain West, 1863–1896* (BYU Press, 1977). He also continued to collaborate with his mentor Leonard Arrington, both in publishing their scholarship and in creating and developing key historical organizations.

In 1965, after Tom had served on BYU's faculty for just over a year, Arrington began efforts to create an association for scholars of Mormon history. Tom participated in preliminary meetings with Arrington, Ellsworth, Allen, Davis Bitton, Richard Bushman, and others, who created an organization called the Mormon History Association.

"We believed that as a field of study the history of Mormonism warranted an organization that focused on that subject," Tom said. He felt this was true not only among Latter-day Saints but for all scholars of religion, considering Mormonism's early communitarian movement, its colonization of the Intermountain West, the ecological and environmental issues the Church experienced in the region, the nineteenth-century conflict with the federal government over theocracy and polygamy, and the Church's missionary system and global growth.

MHA held its first official meeting as an affiliate of the American Historical Association at AHA's conference in San Francisco in December 1965. The small group of about thirty met in conjunction with conferences of the WHA or the Pacific Coast Branch of the AHA for several years until the organization grew large enough to become independent in 1972. Arrington served as MHA's inaugural president. Eight years later, Tom again followed in his mentor's footsteps, becoming MHA's ninth president. Since then, the organization has grown substantially, with some one thousand members—more than thirty-nine percent of them students—several hundred attending annual conferences, and sixteen awards given annually or biennially for work in the field. "I am not sure that any of us understood when we formed the organization in 1965 that it was going to become as large as it is today," Tom said.

MHA played a key role in gaining acceptance for scholarship in Mormon studies in the larger academic community. MHA members publish not only in the organization's quarterly *Journal of Mormon History*, but also in national journals and in scholarly presses. MHA's Smith-Pettit Lecture Series invites leading scholars who are not specialists in Mormon history to look at their field as it relates to Mormon history and share their findings in an annual lecture and corresponding article published in the *Journal of Mormon History*. Tom noted the ability of the organization to bring together those from various faith traditions—or no faith tradition—to engage in Mormon studies dialogue, including scholars such as Jan Shipps, Sarah Barringer Gordon, Larry Foster, Laurie Maffly-Kipp, David Howlett, and Mario DePillis.[8]

In 1972—the same year MHA became independent—Leonard Arrington was simultaneously tapped as the official historian for The Church of Jesus Christ of Latter-day Saints and as director of the newly created Charles Redd Center for Western Studies at BYU.

With these two heavy responsibilities, Arrington asked Tom to serve as his assistant director of the Redd Center. The two consulted regularly, envisioning and planning the center's programs. Because so much work in Western history at that time focused on the Pacific Coast and the Plains, the two decided to define the scope of the Redd Center's interest as the Mountain West.

With Arrington spending most of his time working at Salt Lake City's Church History Department, Tom felt more like the executive director of the Redd Center as he carried out its operations from day one, under Arrington's supervision. In 1980 Tom became the official director of the Redd Center. One of his roles was to fundraise to support the many programs that he and the center wanted to carry out. Tom actually enjoyed fundraising because of the people he was able to associate with, and he left the center in great financial shape to support the interdisciplinary study of the Intermountain West. Today the center funds research, publishing, and public programming by offering awards, grants, and fellowships; hosting seminars and public lectures; and gathering and publishing scholarly materials.[9]

Despite his work directing the Redd Center and his heavy teaching loads, Tom continued to be prolific in his research and writing. I only have space here to touch on a few of his many works, but my fellow essayists will discuss others. With his BYU colleague Jim Allen, he co-authored *Mormons and Gentiles: A History of Salt Lake City* (Boulder, CO: Pruett Publishing Company, 1984) as part of the Western urban history series. Though previous authors had published books on the history of Salt Lake City, the book was groundbreaking because it comprehensively covered the history of the capital city up to the time of the book's publication.[10]

Just two years later, he published *Mormonism in Transition: A History of the Latter-day Saints, 1890–1930* (Urbana: University of Illinois Press, 1986). The book was originally supposed to be part of a "Sesquicentennial History of the Church" series, conceived by Arrington in his role as Church Historian. But the project was stymied when Arrington's open approach to the Mormon past made some church leaders nervous. Authors were left on their own to complete and publish their books. Tom was one of several authors who saw what he started through to fruition. *Mormonism in Transition* won the Mormon History Association's Best Book Award for its groundbreaking examination of the Church's relationship to politics, its development of doctrine, and the effort to deal with polygamy after the Church announced it was abandoning the practice in 1890—in sum, the myriad problems, challenges, and opportunities that the Church faced between then and 1930.[11]

Tom's *Things in Heaven and Earth: The Life and Times of Wilford Woodruff, A Mormon Prophet* (Salt Lake City: Signature Books, 1991) also won the Mormon History Association's Best Book Award, as well as Utah State University's David and Beatrice Evans Biography Award.[12] Tom's work shed new light on the development of the American West

13

and Mormonism during Woodruff's era as the church's fourth president and on how Woodruff's plural family worked even as he grappled with the federal government over polygamy. Tom argued that Woodruff was "the third most important figure in all of LDS Church history after Joseph Smith . . . and Brigham Young."

Tom served as chair of the Redd Center until 1992, when he was appointed the Lemuel Harrison Redd Jr. Professor of Western American History. The chair holder is expected to conduct research and write in the field of Western history, and Tom continued to do so. He held this chair until he retired in 2004 after forty years of service as BYU faculty. Before retiring, he received the Karl G. Maeser Distinguished Faculty Lecturer Award—BYU's highest faculty honor—as well as the Emeriti Alumni Lifetime Achievement Award from Weber State University.[13]

But Tom's years since then can hardly be called retirement. From 2004 to 2005, he and his wife, Marilyn, served a Church Educational System mission for the Church in Berlin, Germany. From 2005 to 2007, he served on the council of the Western History Association. From 2006 to 2008, he served as president of Phi Alpha Theta. He was president of the national organization of the Sons of Utah Pioneers in 2015 and is now on the editorial staff for the organization's publication, *Pioneer Magazine*.[14]

Tom continues to write. One of his most recently published books, *Brigham Young and the Expansion of the Mormon Faith* (Norman: University of Oklahoma Press, 2019), addresses such controversial issues as the Latter-day Saint practice of polygamy, relations and conflicts between Mormon colonizers and Great Basin Indian tribes, and the circumstances and aftermath of the 1857 Mountain Meadows Massacre.[15]

"I'm not happy if I'm not busy," Tom explains. Judging by how busy he has been throughout his more than sixty-year career, he must be a very happy man.[16]

A review of Tom's life and contributions shows three consistent themes—in addition to his hard work and talent—that made his achievement possible: fantastic mentors, open doors, and academic funding. Rather than simply take advantage of these great boons in his own life and career, Tom spent his life doing all he could to pass these opportunities on to others. Besides his many published works, Tom's influence will live on through the numerous students he taught and mentored, who now work in Mormon and Utah history themselves, and through the organizations he founded and led that continue to foster study and scholarship today. In short, Tom's legacy will continue for generations.

As a scholar of Utah and Mormon history myself who has benefitted from Tom's leadership, and on behalf of the Mormon History Association—the organization he helped found which I have had the privilege of leading—I join with countless others in expressing appreciation for Tom's legacy.

Endnotes

1 Thomas G. Alexander biographical page, www.reddcenter.byu.edu; "Thomas G. Alexander," in Alexander L. Baugh and Reid L. Neilson, eds., *Conversations with Mormon Historians* (Salt Lake City, Deseret Book Company, 2015), 1–32.

2 Alexander biographical page, www.reddcenter.byu.edu; Barbara Jones Brown, telephone interview with Thomas G. Alexander, December 11, 2020.

3 "Biographical History," *Register of the Thomas G. Alexander Papers, 1954–2004*, L. Tom Perry Special Collections, Harold B. Lee Library, Brigham Young University; Alexander biographical page, www.reddcenter.byu.edu.

4 Alexander biographical page, www.reddcenter.byu.edu; "Biographical History," *Register of the Thomas G. Alexander Papers*, 1954–2004; "Thomas G. Alexander," in *Conversations with Mormon Historians*.

5 Alexander biographical page, www.reddcenter.byu.edu; "Thomas G. Alexander," in *Conversations with Mormon Historians*.

6 "Biographical History," *Register of the Thomas G. Alexander Papers, 1954–2004*; "Thomas G. Alexander," in *Conversations with Mormon Historians*.

7 Alexander biographical page, www.reddcenter.byu.edu; "Thomas G. Alexander," in *Conversations with Mormon Historians*.

8 For information on the Mormon History Association, see www.mormonhistoryassociation.org; "Thomas G. Alexander," in *Conversations with Mormon Historians*.

9 "Thomas G. Alexander," in *Conversations with Mormon Historians*; BYU Charles Redd Center for Western Studies, "About Our Awards," www.reddcenter.byu.edu.

10 Larry R. Gerlach, "Book Review of Mormons and Gentiles: A History of Salt Lake City," *Utah Historical Quarterly* 53, no. 4 (1985): 396–98.

11 Charles S. Peterson, "Reviewed Work: Mormonism in Transition: A History of the Latter-Day Saints, 1890–1930 by Thomas G. Alexander," *Huntington Library Quarterly* 49, no. 4 (Autumn 1986): 421–23; Alexander biographical page, www.reddcenter.byu.edu.

12 Alexander biographical page, www.reddcenter.byu.edu.

13 "Biographical History," *Register of the Thomas G. Alexander Papers, 1954–2004*; Emeriti Lifetime Achievement Award, www.alumni.weber.edu.

14 Alexander biographical page, www.reddcenter.byu.edu.

15 Megan Stanton, "Review of *Brigham Young and the Expansion of the Mormon Faith*, by Thomas G. Alexander," *Western Historical Quarterly* 51, no. 3 (Autumn 2020), 339–40.

16 "Thomas G. Alexander," in *Conversations with Mormon Historians*.

THOMAS G. ALEXANDER: ENVIRONMENTAL STEWARDSHIP IN THE AMERICAN WEST

Sara Dant, Brady Presidential Distinguished Professor and Chair of History, Weber State University

Assessing the environmental history scholarship of Tom Alexander is at once inspiring and daunting. Having taken time to review Tom's work over the course of a several weeks, I am willing to provide a service to anyone reading this tribute: If at any time you begin to feel a little smug about your publication, service, and community involvement record, please send me a quick email and let me know of your condition. I promise that my reply will be brief, but I will attach for your consideration a copy of Tom's curriculum vitae [see appendix]. He is the author, coauthor, editor, or coeditor of thirty books and monographs and 150 articles as of this moment—stay tuned. I can pretty much guarantee that you will be instantly cured of your smugness and will instead be simultaneously humbled, awed, and motivated.

Tom has been teaching and writing for nearly six decades, and he's not done yet, either. His topics span issues of water, economy, forest management, and Latter-day Saint ("Mormon") leadership and theology, and he is a tireless community servant and volunteer. Quite simply, I would argue that is impossible to find any one person in his field with a comparable concentration of knowledge and understanding. The combination of Tom's dedication to meticulous research combined with his wide-ranging curiosity has me thinking that his home may rival the Smithsonian as an archives repository.

Tom's work does double-duty as innovative writing and scholarship that advances our understanding of the world around us and the ways in which people and nature have interacted over time, as well as serving as an invaluable practical example of how to *write* good history. This is the rare quality of Tom's research and thinking: it is eminently teachable. Using scholars and their writing in my classes has helped my students "see" how to make a historical argument: how to support general statements with specific examples; how to write a clear thesis; and significantly, to remind students to keep in mind their audience: For whom are you writing? Why? Or, as I sometimes say flippantly in class, "So what? Why does a reader need or want to know about this material?" Teaching students how to read good writing is one of the best tools I've found for teaching them how to write well. And Tom's work makes my job much easier and quite a lot more fun.

In order to make this evaluation manageable, I'd like to focus on three articles that I think not only capture the breadth and depth of his contributions to the field of environmental history but also highlight the real value that Tom's scholarship brings to the teaching of history.

I'll begin with Tom's short but effective opening essay in the 1971 *Utah Historical Quarterly* entitled "Toward a Synthetic Interpretation of the Mountain West: Diversity, Isolation, and Cooperation."[1] In his introduction, Tom takes on none other than Walter Prescott Webb and *The Great Plains* to argue that the Mountain West, which Webb included as part of the Plains environment, was far from "treeless" or "level." Uniquely, Tom asserts, west of the 100th meridian, trees cover the mountains and plateaus instead of soon-to-be-cleared agricultural lands. This timber distribution meant that western wood was expensive and inconvenient, but hardly absent. The majority of the country's national forests lie in the Mountain states, which proves this point quite decisively. To correct Webb's misrepresentation that the plains environment extended through the Mountain West, Tom offers an alternative hypothesis to analyze and explain western development by acknowledging the region's striking geographic diversity and widely dispersed natural resources. As he explains, much of the West generally—and certainly the Mountain West in particular—is a place of opposites: aridity and abundant rainfall, treeless expanses and dense forests, fertile and nearly sterile soils. Tom's keen observation here is that the region's resources are in pockets rather than evenly distributed—minerals, timber, farmland, water—so that the environment directly influences settlement. People concentrate where the resources are and vacate or bypass where they are not. Tom's essay also strikes at the heart of Frederick Jackson Turner's assertions of "rugged individualism" and "independence" inspired by the frontier to argue that the environmental reality of the West meant that settlement necessitated cooperation rather than self-reliance.[2] Lest you say to yourself, "Well, these are just the basic tenets of New Western History," let me remind you that Tom wrote this essay in 1971, a full decade before the movement erupted in our discipline. The MacArthur Foundation folks missed Tom's contributions when they were handing out their fellowships.

Invariably, Tom sees Utah as the quintessential West. I swear that Hal Rothman's championing of Las Vegas was modeled on Tom's work, although Hal would never have admitted it. Tom argues that "the history of the development of Utah reads like a chronicle of cooperation," and Tom's scholarship has ensured that Utah's history must always be considered when discussing the West, especially the cooperative element.[3] In 1971, Tom argued that "if the reality of Utah's growth has been a long story of cooperative or corporate development, perhaps this realistic approach will be most important in determining whether Utahns can meet the future environmental problems."[4]

I have found this article to be very useful in class for my students. The assignment we work through is an article critique, and since "Toward a Synthetic Interpretation" is short and direct, it's a good place to start with lower-division classes.

The second of Tom's influential articles that I will discuss is his 1994 "Stewardship and Enterprise: The LDS Church and the Wasatch Oasis Environment, 1847–1930."[5] It is worth noting that this particular article rearranged the furniture in many people's heads about the effect of the environment on western settlement. It's impossible *not* to see how this reality has played out throughout the region as Tom examines the classic struggle between environment and economy. Once again, Utah and Mormon history is at the center of this at-what-cost analysis. Tom begins with an explanation of Latter-day Saint beliefs about faith and nature, outlining that both Joseph Smith and Brigham Young taught that animals and plants possess eternal spirits like humans, and thus only good stewardship leads to salvation. Tom also concedes that these teachings did not always produce tangible results. They were often seen as rhetorical rather than actionable prescriptions.

Building on the ideas set forth in "Synthetic Interpretation," Tom describes the settlement of the Wasatch region as an Oasis settlement—a concentrated abundance of water and rich soils in the midst of a "vast desert badlands."[6] The significant change that the Latter-day Saints brought to this oasis was cooperative irrigation. This model extended also to scarce timber stands, which the Church granted to faithful businesspeople to develop as a communal resource. Unfortunately, as Latter-day Saint settlers integrated into the market, their land management practices became less sacred and more secular. As Tom writes, "business people [sic] had shoved religiously motivated stewardship . . . to the back of the bus."[7] This led to overgrazing, excessive timber harvest, and environmental devastation of watersheds. Tom concludes, "none of the environmentally salutary concepts taught by Joseph Smith and Brigham Young carried sufficient moral force to deflect the siren call of national markets and the secular entrepreneurial tradition."[8] It is a classic tragedy of the commons that Tom characterizes as "well-meaning citizens pursuing markets under a secularized entrepreneurial tradition."[9]

With my students, this article becomes a template for an Oasis Analysis. Students summarize the major points in Tom's article, including the forces that bring about change over time, and then apply it to another Oasis settlement in the West. Once Tom points out the patterns, it's impossible not to see them replicated throughout the region.

The other way to use this article is as a comparative analysis exercise for students to learn how historians revise their work. After reading "Stewardship and Enterprise," students read "Lost Memory and Environmentalism: Mormons on the Wasatch Front, 1847–1930," which appears in *The Earth Will Appear as the Garden of Eden: Essays on Mormon Environmental History*.[10] It is worth noting that this book likely would have never existed without Tom's career, writings, and influence. In "Lost Memory," Tom revisits the relationship between religion and environment to reconsider the "problem of collective memory" regarding "environmental problems and change in the Mormon community." Tom humbly concedes, "I have wondered whether I really got the analysis of motivation right."[11] In this iteration, Tom's focus is less on the "oasis" settlement idea. He argues "that in place of an environmental theology was an emphasis on restoration, atonement, and Zion building."[12] Tom is able to show that Latter-day Saint environmental theology was forgotten or de-emphasized for a time but also that a number of authors have begun to recover and restore these earlier teachings—Hugh Nibley and Marcus Nash, for example. As Tom concludes, "repetition in the community and reinforcement in contemporary society are absolutely necessary" for retaining and recovering "cultural memory of environmentally salutary Christian theology."[13]

Finally, Tom brought his unparalleled expertise and understanding of Utah and Mormon history to bear as an expert witness in a recent court case regarding public access and private property rights on Utah's waterways. Tom's "job" was to describe nineteenth-century Utah residents' and leaders' perspectives—theological, cultural, political, philosophical, etc.—regarding Utahns' ownership and right to use Utah's waters "in place." This usage includes fishing, fur trapping, baptisms, laundering, market waterfowl hunting, swimming, recreating, water-powered mills, installation of irrigation diversion works, etc. I had the privilege of working on this project with Tom, and I can attest that his report is a masterful, highly readable, concise, and completely thorough review of the subject matter. I am hopeful that Tom will make it widely available as a journal publication very soon because it is a tour-de-force integration of the knowledge he has assembled across his lifetime as a scholar. Quite frankly, I know of no one else who could have written what he did. It is worth noting that in the court's final ruling under the heading "Undisputed Facts," the judge wrote simply, "the Court accepts as true all of the historical facts set forth."[14]

Tom Alexander is a true citizen scholar who writes for many audiences and whose work permeates the history of the West, simultaneously at the center and the vanguard.

Endnotes

1 Thomas G. Alexander, "Toward a Synthetic Interpretation of the Mountain West: Diversity, Isolation, and Cooperation," *Utah Historical Quarterly* 39, no. 3 (Summer 1971), 202–06.

2 Frederick Jackson Turner, "The Significance of the Frontier in American History," 1893 Speech, available at https://www.historians.org/aboutahaandmembership/ahahistoryandarchives/historicalarchives/thesignificanceofthefrontierinamericanhistory(1893).

3 Alexander, "Toward a Synthetic Interpretation," 205.

4 Alexander, "Synthetic Interpretation," 206.

5 Thomas G. Alexander, "Stewardship and Enterprise: The LDS Church and the Wasatch Oasis Environment, 1847–1930," *Western Historical Quarterly* 25, no. 3 (Autumn 1994), 340–64.

6 Alexander, "Stewardship and Enterprise," 349.

7 Alexander, "Stewardship and Enterprise," 351.

8 Alexander, "Stewardship and Enterprise," 358.

9 Alexander, "Stewardship and Enterprise," 362.

10 Thomas G. Alexander, "Lost Memory and Environmentalism: Mormons on the Wasatch Front, 1847–1930," in *The Earth Will Appear as the Garden of Eden: Essays on Mormon Environmental History*, Jedediah S. Rogers and Matthew C. Godfrey, eds. (Salt Lake City: University of Utah Press, 2019), 47–68.

11 Alexander, "Lost Memory and Environmentalism," 48.

12 Alexander, "Lost Memory and Environmentalism," 49.

13 Alexander, "Lost Memory and Environmentalism," 68.

14 Judge Derek P. Pullan, "Ruling and Order Granting Defendant VR Acquisitions, LLC's and Defendant State of Utah's Motions for Summary Judgement," *Utah Stream Access Coalition v. VR Acquisitions*, LLC, Case No. 100500558, August 16, 2021, 9.

THOMAS G. ALEXANDER: NATIVE AMERICAN HISTORY AND FUTURE SCHOLARSHIP

Farina Noelani King (Diné), Associate Professor of Native American Studies, University of Oklahoma

More Than Words: Indigenous Land Acknowledgement and Truth Seeking

As a professor emeritus of history at Brigham Young University and the former director of the Charles Redd Center for Western Studies, Thomas Alexander has come to know Provo and Utah Valley not only through his studies, but also on a personal level. Unlike most affiliates and residents of BYU and the surrounding areas, Alexander demonstrates and shares awareness of how Provo and the surrounding region formed through Latter-day Saint colonization and the lives, deaths, and removal of Native Americans and the occupation of their ancestral lands—specifically those of the Utes. Alexander focuses on Latter-day Saint colonizers' perspectives and experiences, but he also offers a window into Native American-Latter-day Saint relationships giving voice to—and perspectives from—Native historical figures.

We need to first acknowledge the homelands of *Noochee* ("the people" in Ute) and of Indigenous peoples who have stewarded the land throughout generations. Utah is home to eight different Native Nations, and Utah Valley is the ancestral homeland of several diverse peoples, including the Timpanogos, Ute, Newe (Shoshone), Goshute, and Paiute people, and we respect their elders and ancestors—*Núu-agha-tuvu-pu̱* (Ute) and Goshute in particular.

I express my gratitude for having had the opportunity to participate in this conversation about Thomas Alexander, who is an exemplary historian of the American West and Mormon history. As a *Diné* scholar, I have read some of his work to better understand Native American and Latter-day Saint entanglements, especially as I have considered my own family's story of conversion to the Latter-day Saint and Diné Latter-day Saint experiences in the twentieth century. Utah's Native American history is inseparable from its Latter-day Saint history, which Alexander's research underscored to me even if he did not explicitly state such a point.

A Career: "It Takes Courage to Be Honest and to Seek Truth"

Some might expect me to assess or comment on Alexander's overarching career, which other scholars could address more fully with details and direct experience. Many people measure a career by a person's work and accomplishments, but it is important to recognize the significance of relationships when assessing a career. Although I focus primarily on one of his recent books, I recognize and commend Alexander for his sensitivity to Native perspectives. I remember the many times that he has gone out of his way to greet me and show support for my work and contributions. He has paid attention and exerted an effort to connect with scholars and learners of all backgrounds. It's meaningful to see his openness to Indigenous methodologies and how he has shown support for Native American and Indigenous scholars. When I was the program co-chair for the Western History Association in 2018 (San Antonio), we featured a Comanche drum group. Alexander approached me to greet me, and I directed him to join a line to shake hands with WHA President Donald Fixico, instead, as the drum group honored him. Alexander followed my directives without question. He has shown a sincere willingness to learn and engage with new peoples and cultures as an emeritus professor and continual scholar.

My comments primarily focus on Alexander's *Brigham Young and the Expansion of the Mormon Faith* (2019) and Young's relation with Natives and the larger American West. Most importantly, I consider how Alexander seeks to fully understand what happened in the past, including in the interactions, relations, and violence between Latter-day Saints and Native Americans—especially Indigenous peoples of what is now known as the state of Utah.

Honesty: A Historian's Virtue

How can we be honest as historians when we look through a distorted lens at times because of the orientation of our own cultural baggage? Scholars need to continue this work and include more conversations with people from different vantage points and positionality.

Alexander presents several key points in the preface of his book *Brigham Young and the Expansion of the Mormon Faith*. He emphasizes how he has sought to balance two traditions: academic scholarship and religious culture. As a Diné Latter-day Saint scholar and historian, I can certainly relate to this balancing act. Unlike Alexander, my Diné identity adds layers to this intersectionality, along with my womanhood.

Considering Maori scholar Gina Colvin's work, specifically in "There's No Such Thing as a Gospel Culture," I have also begun to question whether Mormonism is a culture, including in the way that Alexander refers to it.[1] Rather, Alexander could clarify that he is referring to a European-American culture within the Latter-day Saint faith that has set itself historically as a predominant or "model" culture of Church members. Alexander is open about his faith and recognizes his "cultural baggage" as the descendant and historian of [Utah] "pioneers." He begins his book about Brigham Young with an important foundational point about the study of history itself and perspective: "In several previously published articles, I have argued that objectivity—as scholars generally use the term—is impossible. Every person carries some cultural baggage that no amount of scholarly detachment or persistence can overcome."[2]

Alexander upholds honesty as the historian's virtue: "I have argued and still believe that honesty is the most important virtue historians can seek to achieve."[3] This statement seems simple and straightforward, but honesty in history remains controversial to this day. Although honesty can be ugly and messy, Alexander makes a commitment to seeking the truth of what happened in the past, which is a virtue that Native American history desperately needs. Many histories of Native Americans have been silenced and distorted to fit the dominant celebratory narratives of the United States and those who chose to join the US, as many Latter-day Saint settlers did in the late nineteenth century through the statehood of Utah. In his book, however, Alexander traces "successes" of Brigham Young as a "colonizer."[4] A scholar's questions and positions reveal subjectivities, which Alexander openly refers to in the preface of his book. Some scholars contend whether there is any success in being a colonizer, as success implies positive outcomes. A Native American scholar might rather ask how Brigham Young's colonization affected Native Americans.

The Redd Center and History of the American West

I attended Brigham Young University (BYU) not long after Alexander's retirement in 2004, but his work has certainly affected my interests and understandings of the history of BYU, the Church, and Native Americans. Former Associate Director of the Charles Redd Center Jessie L. Embry launched the LDS Native American Oral History Project in 1989 while Alexander was director of the Redd Center. I later contributed to the project between 2007 and 2008, conducting about one hundred oral histories with Latter-day Saint Native Americans. The Redd Center has supported numerous initiatives and projects relating to Native American Studies, both under Alexander's direction and afterwards. The LDS Native American Oral History Project, for example, led me to pursue oral history as a methodology in Native American history and studies.

Those who have historically benefited from the dispossession of Indigenous peoples have recently been supporting work to understand the realities of that past. For many years, sponsorship of such scholarship was a way to control the narrative by celebrating and honoring "frontiersmen," but there is a recent effort to more critically understand all aspects and perspectives of that history, including the injustices wreaked on Indigenous peoples.

The historical narratives of the "frontier," as historians such as Frederick Jackson Turner and Patricia Nelson Limerick have debated and shaped over generations, are inseparable from the dispossession of Indigenous homelands and displacement of Native peoples in the past and present. Alexander has become a major contributor to these dialogues and studies, especially in terms of understanding colonialism and the expansion of The Church of Jesus Christ of Latter-day Saints.

In 1992, Alexander was named the Lemuel Hardison Redd Jr. Professor of Western American History. A BYU official website explains that Utah philanthropists Charles "Charlie" and Annaley Redd created and named the Endowed Chair in Western American History after Charlie's father, "who settled and developed Mormon communities in southeastern Utah's red rock desert, forests, and mountains and established a successful livestock empire."[5]

Alexander has shaped the field of Western studies by un-erasing and shedding light on complicated but more authentic understandings of the past. A symbol of this erasure in the histories involving Brigham Young that Alexander contributes to is the mysterious daguerreotype of Brigham Young sitting beside a Native woman with her face rubbed out.⁶ The etched-out face of the woman at Young's side—likely Sally Young Knanosh (Bannock), who lived in the Young household as either a servant, adopted daughter, or perhaps even a plural wife—reminds me of all the efforts to erase the complicated and fraught past of Latter-day Saint conquest and settlement in Indigenous homelands in the Intermountain West.

In *On Zion's Mount*, Jared Farmer argued that "paradoxically, the [Latter-day Saints] created their homeland at the expense of the local Indians."⁷ These "Indians" have a name that they called themselves, and they continue to exist. We cannot move past history while we continue to live with its wounds. The voices, perspectives, public memories, and narratives that we perpetuate can either block or promote such healing. Sadly, there have been far more blockages to healing.

Brigham Young and the Expansion of the Mormon Faith addresses such narratives and different perspectives. This work also underlines the ongoing need to include Indigenous voices and sources instead of relying solely upon those of Latter-day Saints and non-Natives. Alexander introduces, for example, Sanpitch and the "imprisonment of hostages" that Young enacted: "The imprisonment of hostages and the subsequent killings poisoned the relations with bands of *friendly* Indians led by Sowiette and Kanosh."⁸ I emphasize the term "friendly" since there has been a historical dichotomization between "friendly" and "wild" Indians from non-Native settler narratives and terms. Instead of considering Sowiette and Kanosh as "friendly Indians" in contrast to "warring" or "hostile Indians," scholars need to recognize the actions of Native Americans as strategies.

Alexander referred to the Circleville Massacre, which is another silenced history: "Following the failure of the hostage policy and the Circleville massacre, Young returned to a peace and vigilance policy."⁹ These examples of violence that affected Native Americans and their homelands relate to the work of Will Bagley in his edited book, *The Whites Want Every Thing: Indian-Mormon Relations, 1847–1877*. Bagley includes sources and references to the murder and mutilation of Old Bishop, a Ute man, in "a process called 'nepoed'" that escalated into the so-called "Battle of Provo River."¹⁰ This massacre resulted in the deaths of unarmed women and children. Latter-day Saint settlers chased Utes from their homes and hunted them into the canyons. This tragedy is the kind of "foundational violence" in American history that Shoshone scholar Ned Blackhawk focused on in his groundbreaking book, *Violence Over the Land*.[11]

Binaries and labels, especially of "good" and "bad" Indians and "hostile" and "friendly" Indians, mask the complexities and intricacies of these histories. They also undermine Indigenous perspectives and lived experiences, since the frame of reference of the binary is based on Indigenous relations to European-American, non-Native settlers and their vantage point.

Alexander's major work on Brigham Young, his experiences, his actions, and his choices that affected Native American lives raises more questions and fruitful areas for future research. What more could be gleaned about Young's "friend" Sanpitch, whom he ordered to be taken hostage during the Black Hawk War? Sanpitch was one of the Ute leaders in the Sanpete Valley in 1866. Ute and Mormon forces clashed, culminating in the forced removal of the Utes to the Uintah Reservation.[12] We have also recently learned more about Sally, "an Indian captive in the house of Brigham Young," in a publication from Virginia Kerns.[13]

The terms "ransom" and "hostage" are part of a framework that we can emphasize to call out this injustice and free ourselves from these exploitative practices and systems that racialization enables. Alexander's work reveals direct instances of hostage policies. It made sense to colonizers to hold Indigenous "hostages" to get what they wanted—while Indigenous peoples were expected to accept the legacies of conquest. Slavery and dispossession continue to manifest themselves in various ways that still affect many people today.

We have a lot to learn to recognize our kinship, our common humanity, and ways to continually heal and grow together. I appreciate scholars like Thomas G. Alexander who have paved a way for others to follow by honestly seeking after and telling the historical truth.

Endnotes

1. Gina Colvin, "There's No Such Thing as a Gospel Culture," *Dialogue: A Journal of Mormon Thought* 50, no. 4 (Winter 2017): 57–70.
2. Thomas Alexander, *Brigham Young and the Expansion of the Mormon Faith* (Norman: University of Oklahoma Press, 2019), location 113 [Kindle edition].
3. Alexander, *Brigham Young and the Expansion of the Mormon Faith*, loc. 121.
4. Alexander, *Brigham Young and the Expansion of the Mormon Faith*, loc. 128.
5. "Lemuel Hardison Redd Jr. Emeritus Professors in Western American History," Charles Redd Center for Western Studies website. Accessed online February 26, 2022. https://reddcenter.byu.edu/Pages/previous-redd-chair-holders.
6. To learn more about this daguerreotype, see Richard Neitzel Holzapfel and Robert F. Schwartz, "A Mysterious Image: Brigham Young with an Unknown Wife," *BYU Studies Quarterly* 41, no. 3 (July 2002): 1–11; and "Exclusive: Brigham Young's secret wife?" Fox 13 News, Salt Lake City, posted September 21, 2012, and last updated September 22, 2012. Accessed online February 26, 2022. https://www.fox13now.com/2012/09/21/exclusive-brigham-youngs-secret-wife.
7. Jared Farmer, *On Zion's Mount: Mormons, Indians, and the American Landscape* (Cambridge: Harvard University Press, 2008).
8. Thomas G. Alexander, *Brigham Young and the Expansion of the Mormon Faith*, loc. 4602 (emphasis added).
9. Ibid., location 4610.
10. Will Bagley, ed., *The Whites Want Every Thing: Indian-Mormon Relations, 1847–1877* (Norman: University of Oklahoma Press, 2019), 122.
11. Ned Blackhawk, *Violence Over the Land: Indians and Empires in the EArly American West* (New Haven: Yale University Press, 2006), 502.
12. Alexander, *Brigham Young and the Expansion of the Mormon Faith*, loc. 4602.
13. Virginia Kerns, *Sally in Three Worlds: An Indian Captive in the House of Brigham Young* (Salt Lake City: University of Utah Press, 2021).

REPLY TO COMMENTS AT THE 2021 WESTERN HISTORY ASSOCIATION CONFERENCE, PORTLAND, OREGON

Thomas G. Alexander, Lemuel Hardison Redd Jr. Professor Emeritus of Western American History at Brigham Young University

Assessing the Career of Historian Thomas G. Alexander

For as long as I can remember, I have been interested in history. Unfortunately, my efforts to major in the field were sidetracked for several years. After graduating from Ogden High School in 1953, I enrolled in Weber Junior College. I had a scholarship in social science, but my father, who was a professor in the engineering department at Weber, put considerable pressure on me to major in engineering.

I graduated from Weber, and after one quarter in engineering at the University of Utah, I was called to serve a mission in Germany for The Church of Jesus Christ of Latter-day Saints in January 1956. I was already disenchanted with engineering. While I was in Germany, I decided that no matter what my father said, I was going to major to history.

I returned to Ogden in August 1958 and went to Weber College to talk with Dr. Dello Dayton, a history professor. Dello had been the faculty advisor for the social unit to which I had belonged. I told him of my decision, and I decided to spend an extra quarter at Weber. I took his course in European History because I thought I would major in European History.

Near the end of the fall quarter, I spoke with Dello again and told him that I planned to continue my education, get a PhD in history, and become a college professor. I asked him for advice about where I should study. He told me that he knew some of the professors at the University of Utah, but he was better acquainted with S. George Ellsworth at Utah State University—both had studied at Berkeley. Dello agreed to write a letter of introduction for me to George, who taught Utah history and Greek and Roman history.

I met George in January 1959 and gave him the letter from Dello, which was very complimentary. I took many of George's classes, including Greek and Roman history classes, Utah history, and a historiography seminar. There was no textbook for Utah history at the time, so he used Leonard Arrington's *Great Basin Kingdom* and Bill Mulder and Russell Mortensen's *Among the Mormons*, but the principal information and interpretations came in his lectures.

I was already an upper division student when I enrolled at Utah State, and they had a program that allowed advanced students to begin working on master's degrees while they finished their bachelor's degrees.

I enrolled in that program and got a teaching assistantship at USU working as Joel Ricks's teaching assistant and grading papers for George.

During the 1958–59 academic year, Leonard Arrington was on leave teaching at the University of Genoa, Italy. I was impressed with his book *Great Basin Kingdom*, and I took his class in American Economic History after he returned to Utah State in fall 1959. Leonard was not an econometrician. He was an economic historian. I got to know him well, and he hired me to do some research and writing for him. In the meantime, I was so impressed with George and Leonard that I had changed my major to United States history, and I decided to specialize in Utah history and Western history. I wrote my master's thesis on the conflict between the Latter-day Saints and the federal judges in Utah territory.

Fortunately, my study of engineering was not an entire bust. Since I had taken a surveying course, I worked for two summers surveying logging roads for the Forest Service, and during the summer of 1959, I surveyed for the Bureau of Reclamation.

In the meantime, I met Marilyn Johns. Marilyn and I first went out on a blind date in March 1959. We had already met through common friends, but we had never dated. She was living in Ogden teaching physical education at South Ogden Junior High School. By any measure, ours was a whirlwind courtship: We became engaged on our third date. We didn't tell anyone until May, and we were married in August 1959. I must say that marrying Marilyn was the smartest thing I ever did. She has been completely supportive of my career as a historian, and we have enjoyed a wonderful life together. I completed my undergraduate program and my master's work during 1959–60, and Marilyn and I left for Berkeley in the fall of 1960. I studied at Berkeley until September 1964.

At Utah State, I had also begun doing research for Leonard. Just before we left for Berkeley, I asked him whether he would hire me again to research and write on an economic history project. He told me that he would. Well, I had not heard from him during the year, so Marilyn and I discussed what sort of work I might do during the summer of 1961. Then one day while I was walking in the Berkeley library, I happened to meet Leonard, who had come from Logan to do research in the Bancroft Library. I reminded him that he had told me he would hire me to do some more research. He said he had received a grant to write histories of Utah's defense installations, and he offered me a position co-authoring the articles with him.

I told Marilyn about Leonard's proposal, and at first she was opposed. It would mean that we would have to return to Utah during the summer. That was one time in our marriage when I insisted that I wanted to take a job she was initially opposed to. I believed publishing with Leonard would further my professional career. Well, I worked several summers with Leonard, except the summers of 1963, when I went to Washington, DC, to do research on my dissertation, and 1964, when I was writing my dissertation. We published a series of co-authored articles on Utah's defense installations in the *Utah Historical Quarterly* and the *Pacific Historical Review*. As a result of Leonard's graciousness, I had five or six articles published under my name before I finished my PhD.

When I was finishing my PhD at Berkeley, I received offers to join the history faculty both at BYU in Provo, Utah, and at Fresno State University in California. This was the other time I insisted on considering a position Marilyn was initially opposed to. When she heard that I might apply at BYU, Marilyn said: "You can't go to BYU, they're the enemy!" After all, we had both graduated from Utah State. Well, I took the job, and Marilyn has become a dyed-in-the-wool Cougar. Her BYU vanity plate has long since declared that she is '4' BYU." She has also earned a master's degree at BYU. I remained in the history department at BYU for forty years.

While at BYU, I taught Utah history and Western history, and I developed a course in American environmental history. I owe a debt of gratitude to a number of people at BYU. Because of Leonard and others, I helped organize the Charles Redd Center for Western Studies and later served as its assistant director, associate director, and director. Others at BYU influenced me and assisted me in my career as well. These include Jim Allen, Ted Warner, and Gene Campbell of the history department, and Deans Martin Hickman and David Magleby. Because of my association with Leonard, George, Gene, Jim, and others, I helped to organize the Mormon History Association.

From 1992 until my retirement, I held an endowed chair at BYU funded in part by the Redd family. For that I owe thanks to Leonard, Dean Martin Hickman, Academic Vice President Stan Albrecht, and several others whose help I am not supposed to know about. Thanks to a faculty committee, BYU also awarded me its highest faculty honor, the Karl G. Maeser Distinguished Faculty Lecturer award.

I could never have achieved much without the help of a number of other people to whom I owe a great debt of gratitude, including Dello Dayton at Weber State and George Ellsworth and Leonard Arrington at Utah State. At Berkeley seminars, I am grateful for the help of Mario DePillis and Clark Spence. Both went to bat for me numerous times, and we have become close friends. Others at Berkeley also went out of their way to help me. They include Walton Bean, Raymond Sontag, and Charles Sellers. Without the help of Raymond Sontag and Charles Sellers, I would never have been able to complete my PhD. I also appreciate the interaction and association with other graduate students at Berkeley. They include Jerry Clarfield, George Giacomini, Roger Sharp, Bill Reuter, and Jim Hitchman. We met weekly in an informal seminar, read the latest important books in American history, and discussed them together.

I appreciate the friendship I have developed with others in the historical field. They are too numerous to mention here, but I must thank Dick Etulain for organizing the WHA session about my work. I appreciate the kind comments of Barbara Brown, Sara Dant, and Farina King. I am also thankful for the opportunities I've had to serve in a number of historical organizations, including president of Phi Alpha Theta (the international history honor society), the Pacific Coast Branch of the American Historical Association, and the Mormon History Association.

I would like to say a few things about my philosophy of history. A number of times people have said to me that they think my historical writing is objective. In some cases, I have merely said "thank you." When I have been really serious about replying, however, I have told them that although I appreciate the compliment, I have to tell them that my writing is not objective because I don't believe that objectivity is possible in the sense that scholars in the social sciences and humanities use the term. In fact, as I wrote in the preface of my biography of Brigham Young, "I believe that those who profess to be objective are self-deluded." I also wrote, "honesty is the most important virtue historians can seek to achieve." Furthermore, "any written history consists of a text written by weaving together evidence found in clearly fragmentary and often messy documents with prose that links the evidence together in a story or narrative. All too often, historians allow rhetoric and supposition to substitute for evidence. If the available evidence used in the narrative does not support the rhetoric and supposition, I believe that the resulting story is suspect at best."[1]

I still believe what I published in 1996: "Given the boundless nature of human imagination, if historians do not restrain themselves by basing their narratives only on information they can verify from the past, they run the very real danger of plying the reader with information and interpretations that cannot possibly be true. This restraint is one [thing]—perhaps the only one—that separates history from fiction."[2]

I would go as far as to say that objectivity in the social sciences and humanities is generally influenced by the cultural and intellectual baggage a scholar carries—I might even go out on a limb and say it always is. At Berkeley, I took a course in philosophy of history from Raymond Sontag. At BYU, I taught historiography, which is an investigation of various philosophies of history and how historians do history. Because of my interest in historiography, I have written a number of essays on the topic, two of which are particularly important as statements of my views that historians cannot be objective.[3]

I would like to address aspects of my work that Barbara, Sara, and Farina commented on. In some ways, I have been doing environmental history since Leonard and I published the first articles on the defense installations. These installations reshaped Utah's economy and landscape and lifted it out of the Great Depression. Sara has mentioned some of the other things that I published in the field, including studies of the Forest Service and examinations of attitudes and practice in the environment. Some of those show both sensitivity to and destructive attitudes toward the world in which we live.

In Utah history, in addition to the general history of the state as Barbara noted, much of my work has focused on the history of The Church of Jesus Christ of Latter-day Saints. These have been works about my own people, the people who made the state in which I have grown up and lived most of my life. In my biography of Brigham Young, I wrote on his principal accomplishments, including establishing more than 350 settlements, assisting in establishing railroads, and building cultural and religious centers in Salt Lake City and throughout the territory. I have won prizes for several of the books and articles, including sharing the David W. and Beatrice C. Evans Annual Biography Award in 1992 and the award for the best book on Mormon History published in the year 1991 for my biography of Wilford Woodruff.

I also considered Brigham Young's relationship with Indigenous peoples, which turned out to be a generally negative experience for them. In my writing, I have tried—not always successfully—to treat America's Indigenous peoples fairly. I thank Farina for her comments. In writing in 1964 about the United States's treatment of Indians in Utah, Idaho, and Arizona, I wrote: "The period [of 1863 to 1896] was . . . characterized by an ideology emphasizing a high degree of cultural imperialism and antipluralism. . . . The experiments at Indian acculturation . . . resulted in disease, death, and disruption, and only now nearly three-quarters of a century later, are Indian tribes beginning to emerge from the results of a federal policy which meant well, but which spelled disaster."[4]

In my biography of Brigham Young, I wrote that Young believed that the Indians were children of Israel and that they were a blessed people entitled to live in peace on their land. On the other hand, he sent out settlement parties to establish towns on Indian lands that the Latter-day Saints did not own. He tried to mitigate this problem by negotiating some treaties with Indians and inviting them to settle near Latter-day Saint towns. The policy of establishing Mormon settlements on Indian land, however, led to wars in Utah Valley, Weber Valley, and Cache Valley, and major conflicts including the Walker War (1853–

54), the Tintic War (1856), and the Black Hawk War (1865–72).

During the Black Hawk War, Young ordered Colonel Warren Snow to imprison Ute Chief Sanpitch and three other Utes as hostages in Manti. Sanpitch was an Elder in The Church of Jesus Christ of Latter-day Saints, and he was one of the Utes who, with the encouragement of the Latter-day Saints, had established his band's settlement near Manti. This imprisonment led to the murder of Sanpitch and his three colleagues. He did nothing to deserve this fate. In 1865, he had joined three other Ute chiefs in asking Young to participate in treaty negotiations at Spanish Fork. At the negotiations, Kanosh, a Pahvant Chief, said, "Brigham is the great captain of all, for he does not get mad when he hears of his brothers and friends being Killed, as the California captains do," referring to the California Volunteers under Patrick Edward Connor. In retrospect, I am offended at some aspects of the history of the relationship of the Euro-American part of my people with the Native American part.[5]

Thanks again to the Western History Association for scheduling the WHA session and to Dick Etulain, Barbara Jones Brown, Sara Dant, and Farina King for participating.

Endnotes

1. Thomas Alexander, *Brigham Young and the Expansion of the Mormon Faith* (Norman: University of Oklahoma Press, 2019).
2. Thomas G. Alexander, "Relativism and Interest in the New Mormon History," *Weber Studies* 13 (Winter 1996): 138
3. These are "Historiography and the New Mormon History: A Historian's Perspective," *Dialogue: A Journal of Mormon Thought* 19 (Fall 1986): 25–49; and "Relativism and Interest in the New Mormon History," *Weber Studies* 13 (Winter 1996): 133–41.
4. Thomas G. Alexander, *A Clash of Interests: Interior Department and Mountain West, 1863–96* (Provo, UT: Brigham Young University Press, 1977), 182.
5. Alexander, *Brigham Young*, 289.

EPILOGUE: BRIEF BIOGRAPHY OF THOMAS GLEN ALEXANDER

Jay H. Buckley, Director, Charles Redd Center for Western Studies, Brigham Young University

Thomas G. Alexander is Lemuel Hardison Redd Jr. Professor Emeritus of Western American History at BYU. Born in Logan, Utah, in 1935 to Glen M. Alexander and Violet Bird, he grew up in Ogden and attended public school there. He earned an associate of science degree from Weber College (1955), bachelor's and master's degrees from Utah State University (1960, 1961), and a PhD in American history from the University of California, Berkeley (1965). In 1959, he married Marilyn Johns of Ogden. They live in Provo and are the parents of five children and six grandchildren.

The BYU Department of History hired Alexander in 1964, and he continued his illustrious career there until his retirement in 2004. Before that, he taught at the University of Nebraska at Kearney; Southern Illinois University Carbondale; the University of California, Berkeley; the University of Utah; and Utah State University. Alexander served as assistant director, associate director, and director of the Charles Redd Center for Western Studies (1972–1992) and currently serves as a board member. Alexander is the author, co-author, editor, or co-editor of thirty books and monographs, more than 150 articles, and numerous reviews. He specializes in Utah history, Western history, American Environmental history, and Mormon history.

Some of his books include *A Clash of Interests: Interior Department and Mountain West, 1863–1896* (1977), *Mormons and Gentiles:*

A History of Salt Lake City (1985) (with James B. Allen), *The Papers of Ulysses S. Grant, Vol 5* (Asst. Ed., 1974), *Mormonism in Transition: A History of the Latter-day Saints, 1890–1930* (1986, 2nd ed. 1996, 3rd ed. 2012), *Things in Heaven and Earth, the Life and Times of Wilford Woodruff, A Mormon Prophet* (1991, 2nd ed 1993), *Utah, the Right Place: The Official Centennial History* (1995, 2nd ed, 1996, 3rd ed. revised, 2003), *Grace and Grandeur: A History of Salt Lake City* (2002), *Historical Dictionary of the Latter-day Saints* (4th ed, 2019) (with Davis Bitton), *Edward Hunter Snow, Pioneer, Educator, Statesman* (2012), *Brigham Young and the Expansion of the Mormon Faith* (2019), and *John A. Widtsoe: Scientist and Theologian, 1872–1952* (2023). He is currently writing a history of the interaction of people and the environment along the Wasatch Front and is authoring his own autobiography.

Alexander has won numerous prizes, including the David and Beatrice Evans Biography Award for *Things in Heaven and Earth*, the Mormon History Association Best Book Award for *Mormonism in Transition* and *Things in Heaven and Earth*, the Mormon History Association Best Article Award (three times), the Utah State Historical Society Best Article Award (twice), the Daughters of the American Revolution History Medal Award, the Award of Merit of the American Association for State and Local History, Phi Kappa Phi Emeritus Life Member, the Western History Association Award of Merit and Honorary Life Membership, and the Mormon History Association's Grace Arrington Award for Historical Excellence. He is a fellow of the Utah State Historical Society and the Utah Academy of Sciences, Arts, and Letters. At BYU he earned the Karl G. Maeser Distinguished Faculty Lectureship award, the university's highest honor for a faculty member.

Professor Alexander has served as president of Phi Alpha Theta (the history national honor society); the American Historical Association–Pacific Coast Branch; the Mormon History Association; the Utah Valley Historical Society; the Utah Academy of Sciences, Arts, and Letters; and the National Society of the Sons of Utah Pioneers. He has served as chair of the Utah Humanities Council, the Utah State Historical Society, and the Provo City Landmarks Commission—along with committees for the Western History Association, the Organization of American Historians, and the American Society for Environmental History. Currently, he serves as parliamentarian of the Western History Association and has served as a member of the Western History Association council.

Active in his community and church, Alexander has also served as a Provo City neighborhood chair, as a member of the Provo City Landmarks Commission, and as a member of the Utah State Capitol Arts Placement Commission. In The Church of Jesus Christ of Latter-day Saints, he has served as a bishop, a branch president, a counselor in three other bishoprics, a stake high counselor, a stake and ward executive secretary, an elders quorum president, a high priests group leader, a Sunday school teacher, a ward historian, and in numerous other positions. He served a Latter-day Saint mission in the West German Mission (1956–1958), and he and his wife Marilyn served as a missionary couple in Berlin, Germany (2004–2005), and again in the Church History Library in Salt Lake City (2005).

CURRICULUM VITAE OF THOMAS G. ALEXANDER

Revised December 2024

Editorial note: I have listed Tom first in coauthored works. —JHB

Personal Data

Born August 8, 1935, Logan, Utah

Elementary and Secondary Education: Ogden, Utah, public schools (1941–1953)

Married Marilyn Johns on August 15, 1959

Higher Education

Associate of Science in Engineering, Weber State College, 1955.

Attended the University of Utah, 1955.

Bachelor of Science in History with a minor in Political Science, Utah State University, 1960.

Master of Science in History, Utah State University, 1961. Thesis: "The Utah Federal Courts and the Areas of Conflict, 1850–1895."

Doctorate in History, University of California at Berkeley, 1965. Dissertation: "The Federal Frontier: Interior Department Financial Policy in Idaho, Utah, and Arizona."

Membership in Professional Organizations

American Historical Association

Organization of American Historians

Western History Association

Utah State Historical Society

Mormon History Association
Pacific Coast Branch–American Historical Association
Utah Academy of Sciences, Arts, and Letters
Utah Valley Historical Society
Phi Alpha Theta
Pi Sigma Alpha
Phi Kappa Phi
John Whitmer Historical Association
Forest History Society
American Society for Environmental History
Utah Westerners
Utah Humanities Council

Listed In
Who's Who in America
Strathmore's Who's Who
Who's Who in the West
Directory of American Scholars
Personalities of the West and Midwest
Outstanding Educators of America
Dictionary of International Biography
Who's Who in American Education
Outstanding People of the 20th Century

Professional Positions
Teaching Assistant, Utah State University, 1959–1960.
Teaching Assistant, University of California, Berkeley, 1963–1964.
Assistant Professor of History, Brigham Young University, 1964–1968.
Visiting Research Professor in Economic History, Utah State University, Summer 1965.
Visiting Instructor, NDEA History Institute, University of Nebraska, Kearney, Summer 1966.
Instructor, Brigham Young University Semester Abroad in Salzburg, Austria, 1968.
Associate Professor of History, Brigham Young University, 1968–1973.
Adjunct Associate Professor of History, Southern Illinois University,

Carbondale, Illinois, 1970–1971.
Assistant Director, The Charles Redd Center for Western Studies, 1972–1973.
Professor of History, Brigham Young University, 1973–2004.
Associate Director, The Charles Redd Center for Western Studies, 1973–1980.
Director, BYU Washington Seminar, Summer 1978, Winter 1981, and Spring 1981.
Director, The Charles Redd Center for Western Studies, 1980–1992.
Member of the Board, The Charles Redd Center for Western Studies, 1992–present.
Adjunct Professor of History, University of Utah, Fall 2003.
Lemuel Hardison Redd Jr. Professor of Western American History, 1992–2004.

Professional Services
American Society for Environmental History: Member of the Committee on the Association Budget, 1990–93; Liaison with the Western History Association, 1991–1995; Member of the Committee on the Rachel Carson Prize, 1992–1993; Chair of the Committee on the Rachel Carson Prize, 1993–94; Member of the Local Arrangements Committee, 1995.
Association of Utah Historians: President, 1983–1985.
Brigham Young University: Member, Graduate Council, 1969–1970; Member, Traffic Appeals Committee, 1968–1970; Member, Archives and Records Management Committee, 1973–1978; Member, Distinguished Faculty Lecture Committee, 1973–1975; History Department Graduate Coordinator, 1972–1981, 1996–2003; Member, University Press Publications Committee, 1976–1979; Member, Faculty Advisory Council, 1979–1982, 2003–2004, Chair 1981–1982; History Department Curriculum Coordinator, 1981–1986; Member of History Department search committee for position in Russian History, 1983; Member of American Heritage 100 committee, ca. 1975–1985; University UNIS Bibliographic Committee, 1983–1985; Chairman of the College of Family, Home, and Social Sciences Promotion and Tenure Committee, 1980–1981,

1986–1991; Member of the History Department Policy Advisory Committee, 1986–1987, 1989–1990, 1992–1994, 2000–2002; Co-chairman of the Program Committee, Sesquicentennial of the British Mission Celebration, 1986–1987; Member, Family and Community History Center Advisory Committee for Public History, 1986–1990; Member, History Department Committee on the 200, 485, 490 Curriculum, 1992; Member of the Charles Redd Center for Western Studies Advisory Board, 1992–present; Member of the College of Family, Home and Social Sciences College Planning and Development Committee, 1994–1997; Chair of the History Department Rank and Status Committee, 1995–1997; Member of the *BYU Studies* Academy, 1997–present; Member of the Committee for Symposium "They Gathered To Zion," 1997; Member of College of Family, Home, and Social Sciences Awards Committee, 1997–1999; Joseph Fielding Smith Institute for Latter-day Saint History, Chair of the 2000 Symposium on the Church in the Early 20th Century; History Department United States History Caucus, 2000, History Department Rank and Status Committee member, 2002–2003.

Courage: A Journal of History, Thought and Action: Member of the Board of Editors, 1972–1973.

Dialogue: A Journal of Mormon Thought: Member of the Editorial Board, 1977–1992; Member of the search committee for a new editor, 1987, 1991–1992, 2002.

Evans Biography Award Committee: Local Committee member, 2001.

Indiana University–Purdue University at Indianapolis: Member of the Core Group for Symposia on the Role of Religion in American Life, 1986–1989.

Mormon History Association: Member of the Organizing Committee, 1965; Member of the Board of Directors, 1970–1973, 1975–1976, First Vice President, 1973–1974; Newsletter Editor, 1973–1974; President, 1974–1975; Program Committee Chairman, 1987; Associate Editor, *The Journal of Mormon History*, 1973–1974; Member of the Nominating Committee, 1976–1979, Chair, 1977–1978; Member of the Program Committee, 1990–1991; Member of the Local Arrangements Committee, 1999; Leonard J. Arrington Award Committee, 2000–2004, 2014–2018; Chair of the Article Awards Committee, 2009–2012; MHA Historian, 2003–present.

National Archives: Member of the Board of Directors of the Denver Records Center Advisory Committee for Archival Affairs, 1969–1971; Member of the Region Eight Archives Advisory Council, 1971–1974.

Organization of American Historians: Member of the Membership Committee, 1972–1995; Member of the Merrill Travel Award Committee, 1999–2000.

Pacific Coast Branch–American Historical Association, Member, W. Turrentine Jackson Award Committee, 1993–1995 (chair 1995); Program Committee Member, 1996, 1997; Local Arrangements Committee Chair for the 2000 meeting in Park City; President-elect, 2000–2001; President, 2001–2002; Member of the Board 2002–2005; Member of the Program Committee, 2003–2004.

Pacific Historical Review, article referee, 1999, 2000, 2003.

Pacific Northwest Quarterly, article referee, 2002.

Papers of Ulysses S. Grant: Assistant Editor for Volume V, 1971–1973.

Phi Alpha Theta–Westerners International: Member of the Dissertation Prize Committee, 1990–1991, Chair, 1992–1996.

Phi Alpha Theta, Member of the Council, 1997–1999; Member of the Advisory Board, 1999–2003, Northwestern Regional Coordinator, 2001–2003; Vice President, 2004–2006; President, 2006–2008; Chair of Advisory Board, 2008–2010; Chair of the Redd Center–Phi Alpha Theta Best Book in Western History Award Committee, 2010–present; Organizing sessions for Phi Alpha Theta at the Pacific Coast Branch, American Historical Association, 2006–present.

Sons of Utah Pioneers, Brigham Young Chapter, Calling Committee, 2009–2011; President-Elect, 2011; President, 2012; Past President, 2013; National Society: President-elect 2014; National President, 2015; National Past President, 2016; Member of the Past President's Council, 2016–present.

State of Utah: Historical and Cultural Sites Review Committee,

1985–1991; State Capitol Art Placement Commission, 2000–2003; Capitol Art Placement Subcommittee of the Capitol Preservation Board, vice-chair, 2003–2004.

Utah Academy of Sciences Arts, and Letters: Member of the Awards Committee 1975–1976, Chairman, 1976; Chairman of the Social Sciences Division, 1980–1982; President-Elect, 1987–1989; President, 1989–1991; Past President, 1991–1993.

Utah Heritage Foundation: Member of the History Committee, 1966–1968.

Utah History Fair: Member of the Advisory Board 1980–1996.

Utah Humanities Council, Member of the Board, 1996–2003; Chairman elect, 2000–2001; Chairman, 2001–2003.

Utah Museum of Art and History, Member of National Advisory Council, 2003–2007.

Utah Preservation/Restoration: Member, Editorial Advisory Board, 1982–1985.

Utah State Historical Society: Member of the Advisory Board of Editors, 1968–1980; Member of the Utah Board of State History, 1979–1991, Chairman/President, 1985–1989; Guest Editor for the Summer, 1971 issue of the *Utah Historical Quarterly* on Reclamation and the Environment in Utah; Member of the Board of State History Rules Drafting Committee, 1990–1991; Member of the Subcommittee of the Board of State History on Outside Contributions, 1990.

Utah Valley Historical Society: Board Member, 1965–1966, 2009–2010; President-elect, 2010–2011; President 2012; President-elect 2016–2017; President 2017–2018; Board member 2018–present.

Western Folklife Center: Member of the Board of Directors, 1988.

Western History Association, Member of the Membership Committee, 1969–1990, 1999–(Chair 1969–1972, 1999–2001); Member of the Awards Committee, 1976–1979 (Chair, 1978–1979); Member of the Site Selection Committee, 1980–1983 (Chair 1982–1983); Parliamentarian of the Business Meeting, 1978–2023, 2014–present; Member of the Local Arrangements Committee, 1982–1983; Member of the Editorial Board of *Western Historical Quarterly*,

1984–1987; Member of the Committee on Revision of the Constitution, 1990–1991; Arrington/Prucha Award Committee: Member, 1999–2003, Chair, 2001–2002; Member of the Program Committee for the 2000 meeting; Member of the Council, 2005–2007; Member of Local Arrangements, 2007–08.

Awards and Grants

American Association for State and Local History: Award of Merit for distinguished service in researching, writing, and promoting state and local history. September 8, 1990.

Brigham Young University: Faculty Research Fellowships, 1966, 1969, 1972; Summer Research Awards, 1967, 1968, 1970, 1977; Graduate School Internship Award, 1973–1974; Research Awards, 1973–1974, 1974–1975, 1978–1979, 1979–1980; College of Family, Home, and Social Sciences Research Awards, 1980, 1981, 1982, 1985, 1986, 1988, 1989, 1990, 1991, 1992, 1993, 1994, 1995, 1996, 1997; Fellowship from the Center for Family and Community History for the study of the Wilford Woodruff family, 1987–1988; Karl G. Maeser Distinguished Faculty Lecturer, 1994; Charles Redd Center Faculty and Independent Research Grants, 1994, 1995, 1998, 2000–2001, 2001–2002, 2010, 2011, 2012, 2013, 2014, 2015, 2016, 2017, 2018, 2019, 2020, 2021, 2022, 2023, 2024; Religious Studies Center Grant, 1995; Russel B. Swensen Lecture, 1996; Joseph Fielding Smith Institute for Latter-day Saint History fellowship, 2000–2001, 2003.

Daughters of the American Revolution: NSDAR American History Medal Award, 1997.

Dialogue: A Journal of Mormon Thought: Award for the best historical article submitted in 1985–1986.

Domingues–Escalante State/Federal Committee: Citation for Service, 1977.

David W. and Beatrice C. Evans Annual Biography Award, 1992.

Edward Hunter Snow Family Organization, Grant to write a biography of Edward Hunter Snow, 2001–2012.

Heritage Media Corporation, Grant for Writing a History of Salt Lake City, 2000–2002.

Historical Department of The Church of Jesus Christ of Latter-day Saints: Fellow, Summer, 1975, Summer, 1976; Editor, 2005–2007.

Juanita Brooks Lecture, Dixie College, 1994.

Mormon History Association: Awards for the Best Article on Mormon History, 1967–1968 (with James B. Allen), 1976, 1980; Award for the best book on Mormon History published in the year, 1986, 1991; Grace Arrington Award for Service to Mormon History, 1990.

National Historical Publications and Records Commission: Fellowship in the Advanced Editing of Documentary Sources in United States History 1970–1971 for work on the Papers of Ulysses S. Grant at Southern Illinois University, Carbondale, Illinois.

National Parks Service, Grant for Writing Histories of Ogden Arsenal and Hill Air Force Base, 1995, 1996.

Signature Books: Grant for writing a biography of Wilford Woodruff, 1985–1989.

Outstanding Educators of America, 1975.

University of California at Berkeley: Travel Grant (Woodrow Wilson Foundation), Committee on Research, 1963.

US Forest Service: Contract through MESA Corporation for a History of the Intermountain Region, 1983–1986; Honorary Forest Service Alumnus, 1986; Cooperative agreement for updating of Regional History, 1993–1997.

Utah Academy of Sciences, Arts, and Letters, Distinguished University Service Award, 1995; Fellow of the Academy, 2000.

Utah Centennial Foundation and Utah State Historical Society: Grant for writing a one volume History of Utah in commemoration of the Centennial of Utah Statehood, 1989, 1990, 1991, 1992, 1993, 1994, 1995.

Utah Humanities Council–Grants in 1975, 1976, 1979–80, 1990.

Utah State Historical Society: The Morris Rosenblatt Award for the outstanding article published in the *Utah Historical Quarterly*, 1968–1969; Fellow of the Society 1979; Distinguished Service Award, 1991; Best Utah History Article Award, 2008.

Weber State University: Dello G. Dayton Memorial Lecture, 1987;

Chritchlow Lecture, 1998. Emeriti Alumni Lifetime Achievement Award, 2001; Fellowship for writing and lecturing on David Eccles, 2005–2006.

Western History Association, Award of Merit, 1999; Honorary Life Member, 2006.

Woodrow Wilson Foundation: Travel Grant, 1963.

Books and Monographs

Alexander, Thomas G., and Leonard Arrington. *Water for Urban Reclamation: The Provo River Project*. Logan, UT: Utah Agricultural Experiment Station, 1966.

Alexander, Thomas G., ed. *The Papers of Ulysses S. Grant*, vol. 5: April 1–August 31, 1962. Carbondale, IL: Southern Illinois University Press, 1973.

Alexander, Thomas G., ed. *Essays on the American West, 1972–1973*. Provo, UT: Brigham Young University Press, 1974.

Alexander, Thomas G., Leonard J. Arrington, and Dean L. May. *A Dependent Commonwealth: Utah's Economy from Statehood to the Great Depression*. Provo, UT: Brigham Young University Press, 1974.

Alexander, Thomas G., and James B. Allen. *Manchester Mormons: The Journal of William Clayton, 1840–1842*. Salt Lake City, UT: Peregrine Smith, Inc., 1974.

Alexander, Thomas G., ed. *Essays on the American West, 1973–74*. Provo, UT: Brigham Young University Press, 1975.

Alexander, Thomas G., ed. *Essays on the American West, 1974–75*. Provo, UT: Brigham Young University Press, 1976.

Alexander, Thomas G. *A Clash of Interests: Interior Department and Mountain West, 1863–96*. Provo, UT: Brigham Young University Press, 1977.

Alexander, Thomas G., Richard D. Poll, Eugene E. Campbell, and David E. Miller, eds. *Utah's History*. Provo, UT: Brigham Young University Press, 1978; 2nd ed. Logan, UT: Utah State University Press, 1989.

Alexander, Thomas G., ed. *"Soul Butter and Hog Wash" and Other Essays on the American West*. Provo, UT: Brigham Young University

Press, 1978.

Alexander, Thomas G., ed. *Voices from the Past: Diaries, Journals, and Autobiographies.* Provo, UT: Campus Education Week, 1980.

Alexander, Thomas G., ed. *The Mormon People: Their Character and Traditions.* Provo, UT: Brigham Young University Press, 1980.

Alexander, Thomas G., and John F. Bluth, eds. *The Twentieth Century American West: Contributions to an Understanding.* Midvale, UT: Charles Redd Center for Western Studies, 1983.

Alexander, Thomas G., and Jessie L. Embry, eds. *After 150 Years: The Latter-day Saints in Sesquicentennial Perspective.* Midvale, UT: Charles Redd Center for Western Studies, 1983.

Alexander, Thomas G., and James B. Allen. *Mormons and Gentiles: A History of Salt Lake City.* Boulder, CO: Pruett Publishing Company, 1984.

Alexander, Thomas G. *Mormonism in Transition: A History of the Latter-day Saints, 1890–1930.* Urbana, IL: University of Illinois Press, 1986; rev. 2nd ed. 1996; rev. 3rd ed., 2012.

Alexander, Thomas G. *The Rise of Multiple-Use Management in the Intermountain West: A History of Region 4 of the Forest Service.* Washington, DC: USDA Forest Service, 1987.

Alexander, Thomas G. *The Forest Service and the LDS Church in the Mid-Twentieth Century: Utah National Forests as a Test Case.* Dello G. Dayton Memorial Lecture 1987. Ogden, UT: Weber State College Press, 1988.

Alexander, Thomas G., ed. *Great Basin Kingdom Revisited: Contemporary Perspectives.* Logan, UT: Utah State University Press, 1991.

Alexander, Thomas G. *Things in Heaven and Earth: The Life and Times of Wilford Woodruff, A Mormon Prophet.* Salt Lake City, UT: Signature Books, 1991; rev. 2nd ed., 1993.

Alexander, Thomas G. *Utah, The Right Place.* Layton, UT: Gibbs Smith, 1995; rev. 2nd ed., 1996; rev. 3rd ed., 2003.

Alexander, Thomas G., and Doug McChristian. *From Arms to Aircraft: A Brief History of Hill Air Force Base.* Hill Air Force Base, UT: Hill Air Force Base, 1996.

Alexander, Thomas G. *Grace and Grandeur: A History of Salt Lake City.*

Carlsbad, CA: Heritage Media Corporation, 2002.

Alexander, Thomas G., ed. *Times of Transition, 1890–1920: Proceedings of the 2000 Symposium of the Joseph Fielding Smith Institute for Latter-day Saint History at Brigham Young University*. Provo, UT: Joseph Fielding Smith Institute for Latter-day Saint History, 2003.

Alexander, Thomas G. *Brigham Young, the Quorum of the Twelve, and the Latter-day Saint Investigation of the Mountain Meadows Massacre*. Leonard J. Arrington Mormon History Lecture Series, no. 12. Logan, UT: Utah State University Merrill Library Special Collections and Archives, 2006.

Alexander, Thomas G., ed. *The Mormon History Association's Tanner Lectures: The First Twenty Years*. Urbana, UT: University of Illinois Press, 2006.

Alexander, Thomas G., and Davis Bitton. *Historical Dictionary of Mormonism*; renamed *Historical Dictionary of the Latter-day Saints*. 4th ed. Lanham, MD: Rowman Littlefield, 2019.

Alexander, Thomas G. *Edward Hunter Snow: Pioneer, Educator, Statesman*. Norman, OK: Arthur H. Clark; University of Oklahoma Press, 2012.

Alexander, Thomas G. *Brigham Young and the Expansion of the Mormon Faith*. Norman, OK: University of Oklahoma Press, 2019.

Alexander, Thomas G. *John A. Widtsoe: Scientist and Theologian, 1872–1952*. Salt Lake City, UT: Signature Books, 2023.

Alexander, Thomas G. *Personal Autobiography*. (work in progress)

Autobiographical References

Baugh, Alexander L. and Reid L. Neilson, eds. "Thomas G. Alexander: Interview by Dave Hall." In *Conversations with Mormon Historians*, 1–32. Provo, UT: Religious Studies Center, Brigham Young University, 2015.

Articles, Book Chapters, and Encyclopedia Entries

Alexander, Thomas G. "From Dearth to Deluge: Utah's Coal Industry." *Utah Historical Quarterly* 31 (Summer 1963): 235–47.

Alexander, Thomas G., and Leonard J. Arrington. "The U.S. Army in Cedar Valley: Camp Floyd Utah, 1858–1861." Presented in mimeographed form to the Western History Association Special Tour, October 17, 1963.

Alexander, Thomas G., and Leonard J. Arrington. "World's Largest Military Reserve: Wendover Air Force Base, 1941–1963." *Utah Historical Quarterly* 31 (Fall 1963): 324–35.

Alexander, Thomas G., and Leonard J. Arrington. "They Kept 'Em Rolling: The Tooele Army Depot, 1942–1962." *Utah Historical Quarterly* 31 (Winter 1963): 3–25.

Alexander, Thomas G., and Leonard J. Arrington. "Supply Hub of the West: Defense Depot Ogden, 1941–1964." *Utah Historical Quarterly* 32 (Spring 1964): 99–121.

Alexander, Thomas G., and Leonard J. Arrington. "The Utah Military Frontier, 1872–1919: Forts Cameron, Thornburgh, and Duchesne." *Utah Historical Quarterly* 32 (Fall 1964): 330–54.

Alexander, Thomas G., and Leonard J. Arrington. "Sentinels on the Desert: The Dugway Proving Ground (1942–1963) and Deseret Chemical Depot (1942–1955)." *Utah Historical Quarterly* 32 (Winter 1964): 32–53.

Alexander, Thomas G., and Leonard J. Arrington. "Utah's First Line of Defense: The Utah National Guard and Camp W. G. Williams, 1926–1965." *Utah Historical Quarterly* 33 (Spring 1964): 141–56.

Alexander, Thomas G., and Leonard J. Arrington. "Utah's Small Arms Ammunition Plant During World War II." *Pacific Historical Review* 34 (May 1965): 185–96.

Alexander, Thomas G. "Ogden's 'Arsenal of Democracy,' 1920–1955." *Utah Historical Quarterly* 33 (Summer 1965): 237–47.

Alexander, Thomas G., and Leonard J. Arrington. "The U.S. Army Overlooks Salt Lake Valley: Fort Douglas, 1862–1965." *Utah Historical Quarterly* 33 (Fall 1965): 326–50.

Alexander, Thomas G., Leonard J. Arrington, and Eugene A. Erb Jr. "Utah's Biggest Business: Ogden Air Material Area at Hill Air Force Base, 1938–1965." *Utah Historical Quarterly* 33 (Winter 1965): 9–33.

Alexander, Thomas G. "Brief Histories of Three Federal Military Installations in Utah: Kearns Army Air Base, Hurricane Mesa, and

Green River Test Complex." *Utah Historical Quarterly* 34 (Spring 1966): 121–37.

Alexander, Thomas G. "The Church and the Law." *Dialogue: A Journal of Mormon Thought* 1 (Summer 1966): 123–28.

Alexander, Thomas G. "Federal Authority Versus Polygamic Theocracy: James B. McKean and the Mormons." *Dialogue: A Journal of Mormon Thought* 1 (Fall 1966): 84–100.

Alexander, Thomas G. "Charles S. Zane, Apostle of the New Era." *Utah Historical Quarterly* 34 (Fall 1966): 290–314.

Alexander, Thomas G., and Leonard J. Arrington. "Camp in the Sagebrush: Camp Floyd, Utah, 1858–1861." *Utah Historical Quarterly* 34 (Winter 1966): 3–21.

Alexander, Thomas G. "The Church and Political, Social, and Economic Issues: An Equivocal Heritage." *Dialogue: A Journal of Mormon Thought* 2 (Autumn 1967): 127–34.

Alexander, Thomas G., and James B. Allen. "The Mormons in the Mountain West: A Selected Bibliography." *Arizona and the West* 9 (Winter 1967): 365–84.

Alexander, Thomas G. "The Powell Irrigation Survey and the People of the Mountain West." *Journal of the West* 7 (January 1968): 48–54.

Alexander, Thomas G. "John Wesley Powell, the Irrigation Survey, and the Inauguration of the Second Phase of Irrigation Development in Utah." *Utah Historical Quarterly* 37 (Spring 1969): 190–206.

Alexander, Thomas G. "Mason Brayman and the Boise Ring." *Idaho Yesterdays* 14 (Fall 1970): 21–27.

Alexander, Thomas G. "An Experiment in Progressive Legislation: The Granting of Woman Suffrage in Utah." *Utah Historical Quarterly*, 38 (Winter 1970): 20–30. Reprinted in *Battle for the Ballot: Essays on Woman Suffrage in Utah, 1870–1896*, edited by Carol Cornwall Madsen. Logan, UT: Utah State University Press, 1997.

Alexander, Thomas G. "Progressive Social Legislation." In *William Spry: Man of Firmness, Governor of Utah* by William L. Roper and Leonard J. Arrington, 87–90. Salt Lake City, UT: University of Utah Press, 1971.

Alexander, Thomas G. "A Conflict of Perceptions: Ulysses S. Grant and the Mormons." *Newsletter of the Ulysses S. Grant Association* 8 (July 1971): 29–42.

Alexander, Thomas G. "Toward a Synthetic Interpretation of the Mountain West: Diversity, Isolation, and Cooperation." *Utah Historical Quarterly* 39 (Summer 1971): 202–6.

Alexander, Thomas G. "An Investment in Progress, Utah's First Reclamation Project, the Strawberry Valley Project." *Utah Historical Quarterly* 39 (Summer 1971): 286–304.

Alexander, Thomas G. "Senator Reed Smoot and Western Land Policy, 1905–1920." *Arizona and the West* 13 (Fall 1971): 245–64.

Alexander, Thomas G. "Reed Smoot, the LDS Church, and Progressive Legislation, 1903–1933." *Dialogue: A Journal of Mormon Thought* 7 (Spring 1972): 47–56.

Alexander, Thomas G. "A Note on the Sources for Utah History in the Denver Records Center." *Utah History Research Bulletin* 1 (Spring 1972): 3–4.

Alexander, Thomas G. "The Federal Land Survey System and the Mountain West, 1870–1896." In *The American Territorial System*, edited by John Porter Bloom, 145–60. Athens, OH: Ohio University Press, 1973.

Alexander, Thomas G. "Ideology and the Development of Environmental Policy." In *Proceedings of the Environmental Law Symposium: Development, Standards and Enforcement*, 7–24. Provo, UT: Brigham Young University, 1974.

Alexander, Thomas G. "Wilford Woodruff and the Changing Nature of Mormon Religious Experience." *Church History* 45 (March 1976): 56–69. Reprint with commentary in *Journal of Mormon History* 43 (April 2017): 46–72. Commentary: "Reflections on My Presidential Address." *Journal of Mormon History* 43 (April 2017): 46–50.

Alexander, Thomas G., and Ted J. Warner. "The Domingues–Escalante Trail from Utah Lake to the Utah–Arizona Boundary, September 25–October 15, 1776." In *The Route of the Domingues–Escalante Expedition, 1776-77*, edited by David E. Miller, 121–43. The Domingues–Escalante State/Federal Committee and the Four Corners Regional Commission, 1976.

Alexander, Thomas G. "Teapot Dome Revisited: Reed Smoot and the Conservation in the 1920s." *Utah Historical Quarterly* 45 (Fall 1977): 352–68.

Alexander, Thomas G. "Political Patterns of Early Statehood, 1896–1919," "Integration into the National Economy, 1896–1920," and "From War to Depression." In *Utah's History*, edited by Richard D. Poll, Thomas G. Alexander, Eugene E. Campbell, and David E. Miller, 409–46, 463–80. Provo, UT: Brigham Young University Press, 1978.

Alexander, Thomas G. "The Place of Joseph Smith in the Development of American Religion: A Historiographical Inquiry." *Journal of Mormon History* 5 (1978): 3–17.

Alexander, Thomas G. "Ogden, A Federal Colony in Utah." *Utah Historical Quarterly* 47 (Summer 1979): 290–309.

Alexander, Thomas G. "The Reconstruction of Mormon Doctrine: From Joseph Smith to Progressive Theology." *Sunstone* 5 (July–August 1980): 24–33. Reprint, 10th Anniversary issue of *Sunstone*, 1985. Republished in slightly altered form in *Line upon Line: Essays on Mormon Doctrine*, edited by Gary James Bergera, 53–56. Salt Lake City, UT: Signature Books, 1989. Reprinted in twenty-fifth anniversary issue: *Sunstone* 22 (June 1999): 15–24.

Alexander, Thomas G. "The Word of Wisdom: From Principle to Requirement." *Dialogue* 14 (Fall 1981): 78–88.

Alexander, Thomas G., and Howard A. Christy. "Utah and the Military Experience." In *Atlas of Utah*, edited by Deon C. Greer, Klaus D. Gurgel, Wayne L. Wahlquist, Howard A. Christy, and Gary B. Peterson, 107–8. Provo, UT: Brigham Young University Press, 1981.

Alexander, Thomas G., and Jessie L. Embry. "Toward a Twentieth-Century Synthesis: The Historiography of Utah and Idaho." *Pacific Historical Review* 50 (November 1981): 475–98.

Alexander, Thomas G. "Utah War Industry during World War II: A Human Impact Analysis." *Utah Historical Quarterly* 51 (Winter 1983): 72–92.

Alexander, Thomas G. "'To Maintain Harmony': Adjusting to External and Internal Stress, 1890–1930." *Dialogue* 15 (Winter 1982): 44–

58. Reprinted in *The New Mormon History*, edited by D. Michael Quinn. Salt Lake City, UT: Signature Books, 1991.

Alexander, Thomas G. "Between Revivalism and the Social Gospel: The Latter-day Saints Social Advisory Committee, 1916–1922." *BYU Studies* 23, no. 1 (January 1983): 19–39.

Alexander, Thomas G. "Toward the New Mormon History: An Examination of the Literature on the Latter-day Saints in the Far West." In *Historians and the American West*, edited by Michael P. Malone, 344–68. Lincoln, NE: University of Nebraska Press, 1983.

Alexander, Thomas G. "Department of Interior." In *Government Agencies*, edited by Donald R. Whitnah, 127–32. Westport, CT: Greenwood Press, 1983.

Alexander, Thomas G. "The Intellectual in the Service of the Faith: The Pursuit of Understanding." *Dialogue* 18 (Spring 1985): 109–11. Translated and republished as: "Das Streben Nach Verständigung." *HLT Forum* 2 (1986): 25–27.

Alexander, Thomas G. "Historiography and the New Mormon History: A Historian's Perspective." *Dialogue* 19 (Fall 1986): 25–49.

Alexander, Thomas G. "The Faith of an Urban Mormon." In *A Thoughtful Faith: Essays on Belief by Mormon Scholars*, edited by Philip L. Barlow, 53–65. Centerville, UT: Canon Press, 1986. Republished in *The Word from Weber County: A Centennial Anthology of our Best Writers*, edited by Bob Sawatzki. Salt Lake City, UT: Friends of the Weber County Library, 1996.

Alexander, Thomas G. "Die Europäische Missionen, 1900–1930: Die Schwierigkeiten, des Evangelium im frühen 20. Jahrhundert zu verbreiten." *HLT Forum* 3 (Früjahr 1987): 45–51.

Alexander, Thomas G. "'A New and Everlasting Covenant': An Approach to the Theology of Joseph Smith." In *New Views of Mormon History: Essays in Honor of Leonard J. Arrington*, edited by Davis Bitton and Maureen Ursenbach Beecher, 43–62. Salt Lake City, UT: University of Utah Press, 1987.

Alexander, Thomas G. "From Rule of Thumb to Scientific Range Management: The Case of the Intermountain Region of the Forest Service." *Western Historical Quarterly* 18 (October 1987): 409–28.

Reprinted in *American Forests: Nature, Culture, and Politics,* edited by Char Miller, 179–94. Lawrence, KS: University Press of Kansas, 1997.

Alexander, Thomas G., and Robert Layton. "Utah, The Beehive State." In *The World Book Encyclopedia,* 20:248–68. Chicago: World Book, Inc., 1988.

Alexander, Thomas G. "Joseph Smith, 1805–1844." In *Research Guide to American Historical Biography,* edited by Robert Muccigrosso, 1404–11. Washington, DC: Beacham Publishing, 1988.

Alexander, Thomas G. "Timber Management, Traditional Forestry, and Multiple-Use Stewardship: The Case of the Intermountain Region, 1950–85." *Journal of Forest History* 33 (January 1988): 21–34.

Alexander, Thomas G. "New Testament Christianity and The Book of Mormon." *Sunstone* 12, no. 4 (July 1988): 6–7.

Alexander, Thomas G. "Newell, Frederick Haynes." In *Historical Dictionary of the Progressive Era, 1890–1920,* edited by John D. Buenker and Edward R. Kantowitcz, 325. New York: Greenwood Press, 1988.

Alexander, Thomas G. "Reed Smoot." In *Historical Dictionary of the Progressive Era, 1890–1920,* edited by John D. Buenker and Edward R. Kantowitcz, 435–36. New York: Greenwood Press, 1988.

Alexander, Thomas G. "Utah." In *Historical Dictionary of the Progressive Era, 1890–1920,* edited by John D. Buenker and Edward R. Kantowitcz, 490. New York: Greenwood Press, 1988.

Alexander, Thomas G. "Water Power Act." In *Historical Dictionary of the Progressive Era, 1890–1920,* edited by John D. Buenker and Edward R. Kantowitcz, 508–9. New York: Greenwood Press, 1988.

Alexander, Thomas G. "The Manifesto: Mormondom's Watershed." *This People* 11 (Fall 1990): 21–27.

Alexander, Thomas G. "Wilford Woodruff, Intellectual Progress, and the Growth of an Amateur Scientific and Technological Tradition in Utah." *Utah Historical Quarterly* 59 (Spring 1991): 164–88.

Alexander, Thomas G. "The Odyssey of a Latter-day Prophet: Wilford Woodruff and the Manifesto of 1890." *Journal of Mormon History* 17 (1991): 169–206.

Alexander, Thomas G., and Ted L. Wilson. "Salt Lake City." In *Encyclopedia of Mormonism*, edited by Daniel H. Ludlow, et al., 3:1250-52. New York: Macmillan, 1991.

Alexander, Thomas G. "Wilford Woodruff and the Mormon Reformation of 1855-57." *Dialogue: A Journal of Mormon Thought* 25 (Summer 1992): 25-39.

Alexander, Thomas G., and David Roy Hall. "State Legislatures in the Twentieth Century." In *Encyclopedia of the American Legislative System*, edited by Joel H. Silbey, et al. New York: Charles Scribner's Sons, 1993.

Alexander, Thomas G., and Tracy L. Alexander. "Whig Party." In *Encyclopedia of the Confederacy*, edited by Richard N. Current, et. al., 4:1708-9. New York: Simon and Schuster, 1993.

Alexander, Thomas G. "Stewardship and Enterprise: The LDS Church and the Wasatch Oasis Environment, 1847-1930." *Western Historical Quarterly* 25 (Autumn 1994): 341-64; Reprinted in *Stewardship and the Creation: LDS Perspectives on the Environment*, edited by George B. Handley, Terry B. Ball, and Steven L. Peck. Provo, UT: Religious Studies Center, Brigham Young University, 2006.

Alexander, Thomas G. "An Apostle in Exile: Wilford Woodruff and the St. George Connection." *Juanita Brooks Lecture Series*. St. George, UT: Dixie College, 1994.

Alexander, Thomas G., and Rick J. Fish. "Conservation and the Environment in Utah." In *Utah History Encyclopedia*, edited by Allan Kent Powell, 113-15. Salt Lake City, UT: University of Utah Press, 1994.

Alexander, Thomas G., and Rick J. Fish. "The Defense Industry of Utah." In *Utah History Encyclopedia*, edited by Allan Kent Powell, 129-32. Salt Lake City, UT: University of Utah Press, 1994.

Alexander, Thomas G., and Rick J. Fish. "The Forest Service in Utah." In *Utah History Encyclopedia*, edited by Allan Kent Powell, 195-96. Salt Lake City, UT: University of Utah Press, 1994.

Alexander, Thomas G. "The Emergence of a Republican Majority in Utah, 1970-1992." In *Politics in the Postwar American West*, by Richard Lowitt, 260-76. Norman, OK: University of Oklahoma

Press, 1995.

Alexander, Thomas G. "Mormon Primitivism and Modernization." In *The Primitive Church in the Modern World*, ed. Richard T. Hughes, 167–96. Urbana, IL: University of Illinois Press, 1995.

Alexander, Thomas G. "Cooperation, Conflict, and Compromise: Women, Men, and the Environment in Salt Lake City, 1890–1930." *BYU Studies* 35, no. 1 (January 1995): 6–46.

Alexander, Thomas G. "Relativism and Interest in the New Mormon History." *Weber Studies* 13 (Winter 1996): 133–41.

Alexander, Thomas G. "Some Meanings of Utah History." *Utah Historical Quarterly* 64 (Spring 1996): 155–67.

Alexander, Thomas G. "Utah's Constitution: A Reflection of the Territorial Experience." *Utah Historical Quarterly* 64 (Summer 1996): 264–81.

Alexander, Thomas G. "Grant, Heber J." In *Encyclopedia of the American West*, edited by Charles Phillips and Alan Axelrod, 2:625. New York: Simon & Schuster Macmillan, 1996.

Alexander, Thomas G. "Kearns, Thomas." In *Encyclopedia of the American West*, edited by Charles Phillips and Alan Axelrod, 2:808. New York: Simon & Schuster Macmillan, 1996.

Alexander, Thomas G. "Salt Lake City, Utah." In *Encyclopedia of the American West*, edited by Charles Phillips and Alan Axelrod, 3:1412–14. New York: Simon & Schuster Macmillan, 1996.

Alexander, Thomas G. "*United States v. Reynolds.*" In *Encyclopedia of the American West*, edited by Charles Phillips and Alan Axelrod, 4:1664. New York: Simon & Schuster Macmillan, 1996.

Alexander, Thomas G. "Woodruff, Wilford." In *Encyclopedia of the American West*, edited by Charles Phillips and Alan Axelrod, 4:1777–78. New York: Simon & Schuster Macmillan, 1996.

Alexander, Thomas G. "YX Company." In *Encyclopedia of the American West*, edited by Charles Phillips and Alan Axelrod, 4:1808. New York: Simon & Schuster Macmillan, 1996.

Alexander, Thomas G. "The Transformation of Utah from a Colony of Wall Street to a Colony of Washington." *The Thetean* 25 (1996): 1–29.

Alexander, Thomas G. "Reflections on Utah's Kingdom, Colony, and Commonwealth." *Rough Draft* [Friends of the Weber County Library] 17 (Winter 1997): 28–31.

Alexander, Thomas G. "Keeping Company with Wilford Woodruff." *Journal of Mormon History* 23 (Fall 1997): 210–26.

Alexander, Thomas G. "Brigham Young University," "Juanita Brooks (with Leonard J. Arrington)," "George Henry Dern (with Leonard J. Arrington)," "State of Deseret (with Leonard J. Arrington)," "Lake Bonneville (with Leonard J. Arrington)," David Oman McKay," "Orson Pratt," "Provo, Utah (with Leonard J. Arrington)," "Brigham Henry Roberts (with Leonard J. Arrington)," "Reed Smoot (with Leonard J. Arrington)," United Order of Enoch (with Leonard J. Arrington)," and "Wilford Woodruff (with Leonard J. Arrington)." In *The New Encyclopedia of the American West*, edited by Howard R. Lamar. New Haven, CT: Yale University Press, 1998.

Alexander, Thomas G. "Latter-day Saints, Utahns, and the Environment: A Personal Perspective." In *New Genesis: A Mormon Reader on Land and Community*, edited by Terry Tempest Williams, William B. Smart, and Gibbs M. Smith. Layton, UT: Gibbs Smith, 1998.

Alexander, Thomas G. "Kimball, Spencer Wooley" and "Marriott, J(ohn) Willard." In *The Scribner Encyclopedia of American Lives*, vol. 1, 1981–1985, edited by Kenneth T. Jackson, Karen Markoe, and Arnold Markoe. New York: Charles Scribner's Sons, 1998.

Alexander, Thomas G. "Sylvester Q. Cannon and the Revival of Environmental Consciousness in the Mormon Community." *Environmental History* 3 (October 1998): 488–507.

Alexander, Thomas G. "In Remembrance, Leonard J. Arrington." *Newsletter of the Western History Association* (Spring 1999), 5.

Alexander, Thomas G. "Jesse Knight Left Mark on Provo." *Daily Herald* (Provo), May 10, 1999.

Alexander, Thomas G. "Leonard James Arrington." *OAH Newsletter* 27 (May 1999): 23–24.

Alexander, Thomas G. "Remembering Leonard." *Journal of Mormon History* 25 (Spring 1999): 20–22.

Alexander, Thomas G. "Kimball, Heber Chase." In *American National Biography*, edited by John A. Garraty and Mark C. Carnes, 12:677–678. New York: Oxford University Press, 1999.

Alexander, Thomas G. "Smith, Joseph Fielding." In *American National Biography*, edited by John A. Garraty and Mark C. Carnes, 20:235–36. New York: Oxford University Press, 1999.

Alexander, Thomas G. "Woodruff, Wilford." In *American National Biography*, edited by John A. Garraty and Mark C. Carnes, 23:808–810. New York: Oxford University Press, 1999.

Alexander, Thomas G. "Growth, Change Followed World War II." *Daily Herald* (Provo), November 18, 1999, 6.

Alexander, Thomas G. "National Woes Hit Utah Hard in '30s." *Daily Herald* (Provo), November 18, 1999, 6.

Alexander, Thomas G. "Hill Air Force Base Built on Strategic Site." *Daily Herald* (Provo) November 18, 1999, 8.

Alexander, Thomas G. "The Progressive Struggle to Reform the American Democratic Republic." In *Fulfilling the Founding: A Reader for American Heritage*, edited by Gary Daynes, 165–84. Needham Heights, MA: Pearson Custom Publishing, 1999.

Alexander, Thomas G. "Nineteen Years Later." *Sunstone* 22 (June 1999): 24–27.

Alexander, Thomas G. "Wilford Woodruff and Zion's Camp: Baptism by Fire and the Spiritual Confirmation of a Future Prophet." *BYU Studies* 39, no. 1 (January 2000): 130–46.

Alexander, Thomas G. "The Conservative and Conservation: Senator Reed Smoot and America's Public Lands, 1903–1933." *Beehive History* 26 (2000): 22–25.

Alexander, Thomas G. "Leonard J. Arrington," "Sylvester Q. Cannon," "Liberal Party," "Manifesto of 1890," "Political Manifesto," "Second Manifesto," "Mormon History Association," "New Deal," "Salt Lake City," "Utah Statehood," "Ulysses S. Grant," "Utah," "Wilford Woodruff," and "Charles S. Zane." In *Encyclopedia of Latter-day Saint History*, edited by Arnold K. Garr, Donald Q. Cannon, and Richard O. Cowan. Salt Lake City, UT: Deseret Book, 2000.

Alexander, Thomas G. "Hunter, Howard William" and "Lee, J(oseph)

Bracken ('Brack')." In *The Scribner Encyclopedia of American Lives*, edited by Kenneth T. Jackson, 1994–1996, vol. 4: 260–62, 328–30. New York: Charles Scribner's Sons, 2001.

Alexander, Thomas G. "Utah and Mormonism." In *Encyclopedia of American Cultural & Intellectual History*, edited by Mary Kupiec Cayton and Peter W. Williams, 2:655–64. New York: Charles Scribner's Sons, 2001.

Alexander, Thomas G. "Struggle in an Endangered Empire: The Search for Total Ecosystem Management in the Forests of Southern Utah, 1976–1999." In *Forests Under Fire: A Century of Ecosystem Mismanagement in the Southwest*, edited by Christopher J. Huggard and Arthur R. Gomez. Tucson: University of Arizona Press, 2001.

Alexander, Thomas G. "Arrington, Leonard James." In *The Scribner Encyclopedia of American Lives*, edited by Kenneth T. Jackson, 5:20–21. New York: Charles Scribner's Sons, 2002.

Alexander, Thomas G. "Watering the Mormon Heartland: Irrigation Companies and Modernization in Utah's Wasatch Oasis, 1870–1930." *Bureau of Reclamation History Symposium* (CD publication), June 18–19, 2002.

Alexander, Thomas G. "Irrigating the Mormon Heartland: The Operation of the Irrigation Companies in Wasatch Oasis Communities, 1847–1880." *Agricultural History* 76 (Spring 2002): 172–87.

Alexander, Thomas G. "Red Rock and Grey Stone, Reed Smoot, the Establishment of Zion and Bryce National Parks and the Rebuilding of Downtown Washington, D.C." *Pacific Historical Review* 72 (Spring 2003): 1–38.

Alexander, Thomas G. "Interdependence and Change: Mutual Irrigation Companies in Utah's Wasatch Oasis in an Age of Modernization, 1870–1930." *Utah Historical Quarterly* 71 (Fall 2003): 292–314.

Alexander, Thomas G. "Interdependence in the Mormon Heartland: Mutual Irrigation Companies and Modernization in Utah's Wasatch Oasis, 1870–1930." *The Mining History Journal: The Tenth Annual Journal of the Mining History Association* (2003–2004): 87–102.

Alexander, Thomas G. "Church of Jesus Christ of Latter-day Saints." In *Encyclopedia of Religion and Nature*, edited by Bron R. Taylor, 385–88. London: Thoemmes Continuum, 2005.

Alexander, Thomas G. "Church and Community: Latter-day Saint Women in the Progressive Era." In *New Scholarship on Latter-day Saint Women in the Twentieth Century*, edited by Carol Cornwall Madsen and Cherry B. Silver, 9–18. Provo, UT: Joseph Fielding Smith Institute for Latter–day Saint History, 2005.

Alexander, Thomas G. "Generating Wealth from the Earth." In *From the Ground Up: The History of Mining in Utah*, edited by Colleen Whitley. Logan, UT: Utah State University Press, 2006.

Alexander, Thomas G. "Introduction." In *The Notebooks and Letters of William E. McLellin, 1854–1880*, edited by Stan Larson. Salt Lake City, UT: Signature Books, 2007.

Alexander, Thomas G. "Brigham Young, The Quorum of the Twelve, and the Latter-day Saint Investigation of the Mountain Meadows Massacre." Leonard J. Arrington Mormon History Lecture Series, No. 12. Logan, UT: Utah State University Press, 2007.

Alexander, Thomas G. "Review Essay: Revisiting the American West." *New Mexico Historical Review* 82 (Summer 2007): 391–96.

Alexander, Thomas G. "Mormon Prophets and the Environment: Creation, Sin, the Fall, Redemption, and the Millennium." In *Dreams, Myths, & Reality: Utah and the American West: The Critchlow Lectures at Weber State University*, edited by William Thomas Allison and Susan J. Matt, 85–103. Salt Lake City, UT: Signature Books, 2008.

Alexander, Thomas G. "Brigham Young." In *Icons of the American West: From Cowgirls to Silicon Valley*, edited by Gordon Morris Bakken, 1:305–28. Westwood, CT: Greenwood Press, 2008.

Alexander, Thomas G. "Honest History: A Conversation with Thomas G. Alexander." Interviewed by David R. Hall, *Mormon Historical Studies* 8 (Fall 2007): 108–35.

Alexander, Thomas G. "Carpetbaggers, Reprobates, and Liars: Federal Judges and the Utah War (1857–58)." *The Historian* 70 (Summer 2008): 208–38.

Alexander, Thomas G. "David Eccles and the Origins of Utah Construction Company–Utah International." *Utah Historical Quarterly* 77 (Winter 2009): 4–25.

Alexander, Thomas G. "Thomas L. Kane and the Mormon Problem in National Politics." In *Col Thomas L. Kane and the Mormons*, edited by David J. Whittaker, 57–88. Provo, UT: *BYU Studies*, 2010. Previously published in *BYU Studies* 48, no. 4 (October 2009): 57–88.

Alexander, Thomas G. "Transition: 1890–1941." In *Mormonism: A Historical Encyclopedia*, edited by W. Paul Reeve and Ardis E. Parshall, 45–55. Santa Barbara, CA: ABC Clio, 2010.

Alexander, Thomas G. "Wilford Woodruff." In *Mormonism: A Historical Encyclopedia*, edited by W. Paul Reeve and Ardis E. Parshall, 216–19. Santa Barbara, CA: ABC Clio, 2010.

Alexander, Thomas G. "The Odyssey of a Latter-day Prophet: Wilford Woodruff and the Manifesto of 1890." In *Banner of the Gospel: Wilford Woodruff*, edited by Alexander L. Baugh and Susan Easton Black, 277–325. Provo, UT: Religious Studies Center & Salt Lake City, UT: Deseret Book, 2010.

Alexander, Thomas G. "Muckrakers vs. Mormons: A Saga of the Progressive Movement." In *Cartoonists and Muckrakers: Selected Media Images of Mormonism During the Progressive Era*, edited by Michael Harold Paulos and Kenneth L. Cannon II. Salt Lake City, UT: privately printed, 2011.

Alexander, Thomas G. "Conflict and Fraud: Utah Public Land Surveys, 1855–57, and the Subsequent Investigation." *Utah Historical Quarterly* 80 (Spring 2012): 108–31.

Alexander, Thomas G. "Colonies and Settlements to 1857." In *History of the Saints*, edited by Glenn Rawson, Dennis Lyman, Bryant Bush, and William G. Hartley, 197–221. American Fork, UT: Covenant Communications, 2012.

Alexander, Thomas G. "Settling and Colonizing the American West." In *History of the Saints*, edited by Glenn Rawson, Dennis Lyman, Bryant Bush, and William G. Hartley, 259–77. American Fork, UT: Covenant Communications, 2012.

Alexander, Thomas G. "Settling the Wasatch Front." In *Mapping Mor-*

monism: An Atlas of Latter-day Saint History, edited by Brandon S. Plewe, S. Kent Brown, Donald Q. Cannon, and Richard H. Jackson, 88–89. Provo, UT: Brigham Young University Press, 2012.

Alexander, Thomas G. "Brigham Young and the Transformation of Utah Wilderness, 1847–58." *Journal of Mormon History* 41 (January 2015): 103–24.

Alexander, Thomas G. "Reflections on My Presidential Address." *Journal of Mormon History* 43 (April 2017): 46–50. Proceeding reprint of "Wilford Woodruff and the Changing Nature of Mormon Religious Experience." *Journal of Mormon History* 43 (April 2017): 51–72.

Alexander, Thomas G. "Pioneer Vignette: Anthony W. Ivins and the LDS Colonies in Mexico." *Pioneer* 65, no. 1 (2018): 40–41.

Alexander, Thomas G. "Conflict, Tragedy, and Peace: The Utah War, 1857–58." *Pioneer* 65, no. 3 (2018): 4–19.

Alexander, Thomas G. "Wilford Woodruff, Latter-day Saint Missionaries, and the British Mission of 1839–41." *Pioneer* 65 no. 4 (2018): 28–36.

Alexander, Thomas G. "Spanning the Nation: Brigham Young and the Construction of the Transcontinental Railroad." *Pioneer* 66, no. 3 (2019): 20–38.

Alexander, Thomas G. "Drafting the Utah State Constitution of 1895–96." *Pioneer* 67 no. 4 (2020): 23–37.

Alexander, Thomas G. "History of the Interaction of People and the Environment along the Wasatch Front." (work in progress)

Reviews

Review of *Nevada's 20th Century Mining Boom* by Russell R. Elliott. *Utah Historical Quarterly* 35 (Spring 1967): 175–76.

Review of *Orrin Porter Rockwell: Man of God, Son of Thunder* by Harold Schindler. *BYU Studies* 8 (Autumn 1967): 100–2 and *Pacific Historical Review* 38 (February 1969): 101–2.

Review of *The Armies of God* by Paul Bailey. *Arizona and the West* 11 (Summer 1969): 195–96.

Review of *Uranium Fever or No Talk Under $1 Million* by Raymond W. Taylor and Samuel W. Taylor. *BYU Studies* 11 (Autumn 1970):

114–16.

Review of *Ulysses S. Grant* by John A. Carpenter. *Newsletter of the Ulysses S. Grant Association* 11 (April 1972): 19–20.

Review of *Geology and Politics in Frontier Texas, 1845–1909* by Walter Keene Ferguson. *Montana: The Magazine of Western History* 20 (Spring 1970): 76.

Review of *How the U.S. Cavalry Saved Our National Parks* by H. Duane Hampton. *Choice* 9 (July–August 1972): 712.

Review of *Life in the Far West: Among the Indians and the Mountain Men, 1846–47* by George A. F. Ruxton. *Choice* 10 (September 1973): 1069.

Review of *Mormon Battalion Trail Guide* by Charles S. Peterson, John F. Yurtinus, David E. Atkinson and A. Kent Powell. *Nevada Historical Society Quarterly* 16 (Spring 1973): 30–31.

Review of *The Americanization of Utah for Statehood* by Gustive O. Larson. "On Utah's Struggle to be Accepted by Victorian America." *BYU Today* 27 (December 1973): 10–11.

Review of *Adventures in Mexico and the Rocky Mountains* by George Frederick Augustus Ruxton. *Choice* 10 (December 1973): 1622.

Review of *The American West in the Twentieth Century: A Short History of an Urban Oasis* by Gerald D. Nash. *Utah Historical Quarterly* 41 (Fall 1973): 414–15 and *Western Historical Quarterly* 5 (April 1974): 196–97.

Review of *George W. P. Hunt and His Arizona* by John S. Goff. *Arizona and the West* 16 (Autumn 1974): 287–88.

Review of *Dear Ellen: Two Mormon Women and Their Letters*, edited by Ellen Pratt McGary, Ellen Spencer Clawson, and S. George Ellsworth and *Letters of Long Ago* by Agnes Just Reid. *BYU Studies* 15 (Spring 1975): 375–78.

Review of *A Biography of Ezra Thompson Clark* by Annie Clark Tanner. *BYU Studies* 16 (Winter 1976): 303–4.

Review of *The Psychological and Ethical Aspects of Mormon Group Life* by Ephraim E. Ericksen. *Utah Libraries* 18 (1976): 40–42.

Review of *Carthage Conspiracy: The Trial of the Accused Assassins of Joseph Smith* by Dallin H. Oaks and Marvin S. Hill. *Choice* 15 (May

1976): 277.

Review of *Nauvoo: The City of Joseph* by David E. Miller and Della S. Miller. *Utah Libraries* 19 (Spring 1976): 52–53.

Review of *Look to the Mountains: Southeastern Utah and the La Sal National Forest* by Charles S. Peterson. *Pacific Historical Review* 46 (February 1977): 135–36.

Review of *Montana: A History of Two Centuries* by Michael P. Malone and Richard B. Roeder. *Choice* 14 (April 1977): 637–38.

Review of *The Gentile Comes to Cache Valley* by A. J. Simmonds. *BYU Studies* 17 (Winter 1977): 252–53.

Review of *Pioneer Steelmaker in the West: The Colorado Fuel and Iron Company, 1892–1903* by H. Lee Scamehorn. *Western Historical Quarterly* 8 (October 1977): 471.

Review of *Pioneer Steelmaker in the West: The Colorado Fuel and Iron Company, 1892–1903* by H. Lee Scamehorn. *Journal of American History* 64 (December 1977): 805–7.

Review of *Wyoming: A Bicentennial History* by Taft Alfred Larson. *Choice* 15 (January 1978): 611.

Review of *Utah: A Bicentennial History* by Charles S. Peterson. *Choice* 15 (March 1978): 670.

Review of *Joseph Smith: The First Mormon* by Donna Hill. *American Historical Review* 83 (April 1978): 517–18.

Review of *Guide to Mormon Diaries and Autobiographies* by Davis Bitton. *BYU Today* 32 (September 1978): 5.

Review of *Montana: Images of the Past* by William E. Farr and K. Ross Toole. *Choice* 16 (March 1979): 598.

Review of *Along the Ramparts of the Tetons: The Saga of Jackson Hole, Wyoming* by Robert B. Betts. *Choice* 16 (June 1979): 671.

Review of *The Utah Photographs of George Edward Anderson* edited by Rell G. Francis. *Choice* (April 1980): 572.

Review of *Alaska* by William R. Hunt; *California* by David S. Lavender; *Idaho* by F. Ross Peterson; *Montana* by Clark C. Spence; *Oregon* by Gordon B. Dodds; *Nevada* by Robert Laxalt; *Utah* by Charles S. Peterson; *Washington* by Norman H. Clark; and *Wyoming* by T. A. Larson. *American Historical Review* 85 (June 1980): 709–11.

Review of *North to Montana!: Jehus, Bullwhackers, and Mule Skinners on the Montana Trail* by Betty M. Madsen and Brigham D. Madsen. *Choice* 18 (January 1981): 673.

Review of *The Utah Photographs of George Edward Anderson* by Rell G. Francis. *Journal of the West* 19 (October 1980): 85.

Review of *Diary of Brigham Young, 1957* by Everett L. Cooley. *Montana: The Magazine of Western History* 31 (Summer 1981): 74.

Review of *Defender of the Faith: The B. H. Roberts Story* by Truman G. Madsen. *BYU Studies* 21 (Spring 1981): 248–50.

Review of *Reclaiming the American West: An Historiography and Guide* by Lawrence B. Lee. *Pacific Historical Review* 50 (August 1981): 368–69.

Review of *That Awesome Space: Human Interaction with the Intermountain Landscape* edited by E. Richard Hart. *Utah Endowment for the Humanities News and Information* (December 1981): np.

Review of *The Saints and the Union: Utah Territory During the Civil War* by E. B. Long. *Choice* 18 (November 1981): 560.

Review of *The Saints and the Union: Utah Territory During the Civil War* by E. B. Long. *Arizona and the West* 23 (Winter 1981): 386–88.

Review of *F. Jay Haynes: Photographer* by Montana Historical Society. *Choice* 19 (March 1982): 608.

Review of *Rocky Mountain Carpetbaggers: Idaho's Territorial Governors, 1863–1890* by Ronald H. Limbaugh. *Choice* 19 (November 1982): 686.

Review of *From Prophet to Son: Advice of Joseph F. Smith to his Missionary Sons* edited by Hyrum M. Smith III and Scott G. Kenney. *Sunstone Review* 2 (1983): 23.

Review of *The Plains Across* by John D. Unruh. *Journal of Historical Geography* 6 (July 1980): 355–56.

Review of *Heber C. Kimball: Mormon Patriarch and Pioneer* by Stanley B. Kimball. *Journal of the West* 21 (October 1982): 90–91.

Review of *Mormon Thunder: A Documentary History of Jedediah Morgan Grant* by Gene A. Sessions. *Choice* 20 (January 1983): 229–30.

Review of *Apaches & Longhorns: The Reminiscences of Will C. Barnes* edited by Frank C. Lockwood. *Choice* 20 (March 1983): 631.

Review of *The Politics of Wilderness Preservation* by Craig W. Allin and *Crucible for Conservation: The Creation of Grand Teton National Park* by Robert W. Righter. *American Historical Review* 88 (June 1983): 759-60.

Review of *Visionaries, Mountain Men & Empire Builders: They Made a Difference* by Fred Lockley. *Choice* 20 (September 1983): 595.

Review of *Let 'Em Holler: A Political Biography of J. Bracken Lee* by Dennis Lythgoe. *Pacific Historian* 27 (Fall 1983): 73-74.

Review of *Quicksand and Cactus: A Memoir of the Southern Mormon Frontier* by Juanita Brooks. *Choice* 20 (October 1983): 543.

Review of *Mormonism and the American Experience* by Klaus J. Hansen. *Dialogue* 16 (Winter 1983): 146-48.

Review of *Gold Rush Sojourners in Great Salt Lake City, 1849-1850* by Brigham D. Madsen. *Utah Humanities News* (March 1984): 3.

Review of *Rocky Mountain Carpetbaggers: Idaho's Territorial Governors, 1863-1890* by Ronald H. Limbaugh. *Pacific Historical Review* 53 (May 1984): 228-30.

Review of *David T. Mason: Forestry Advocate* by Elmo Richardson. *Montana: The Magazine of Western History* 34 (Spring 1984): 71.

Review of *Tahoe: An Environmental History* by Douglas H. Strong. *Choice* 21 (November 1984): 606.

Review of *Woods-working Women: Sexual Integration in the U.S. Forest Service* by Elaine Pitt Enarson. *Choice* 21 (November 1984): 673.

Review of *Forging New Rights in Western Waters* by Robert G. Dunbar. *Western Historical Quarterly* 16 (January 1985): 86-87.

Review of *History of Sustained Yield Forestry: A Symposium* by Harold K. Steen. *Western Historical Quarterly* 16 (April 1985): 220-21.

Review of *The Carving of Mount Rushmore* by Rex Alan Smith. *Choice* 22 (September 1985): 545.

Review of *National Parks for a New Generation: Visions, Realities, Prospects: A Report from the Conservation Foundation* by Conservation Foundation. *Choice* 22 (October 1985): 471.

Review of *Mormonism: The Story of a New Religious Tradition* by Jan Shipps. *Dialogue: A Journal of Mormon Thought* 18 (Winter 1985):

185–87.

Review of *The New Deal and the West* by Richard Lowitt. *Technology and Culture* 27 (January 1986): 164–65.

Review of *Theodore Roosevelt, the Making of a Conservationist* by Paul Russell Cutright. *Choice* 23 (April 1986): 491.

Review of *The American West Transformed: The Impact of the Second World War* by Gerald D. Nash. *Indiana Magazine of History* 82 (June 1986): 215–16.

Review of *U.S. Forest Service Grazing and Rangelands: A History* by William D. Rowley. *Western Historical Quarterly* 17 (July 1986): 340–41.

Review of *Brigham Young: American Moses* by Leonard J. Arrington. *Pacific Historian* 30 (Spring 1986): 64-65.

Review of *Emma Lee* by Juanita Brooks. *Pacific Historical Review* 55 (November 1986): 623.

Review of *The 1838 Mormon War in Missouri* by Stephen C. LeSueur. *Choice* 24 (October 1987): 562.

Review of *The Mormon Corporate Empire* by John Heinerman and Anson Shupe. *Journal for the Scientific Study of Religion* 26 (September 1987): 417–18.

Review of *Missionary to the Mountain West: Reminiscences of Episcopal Bishop Daniel S. Tuttle, 1866-1886* by Daniel Sylvester Tuttle. *Utah Historical Quarterly* 56 (Spring 1988): 198–99.

Review of *Mormons at the Missouri, 1846-1852: "and should we die..."* by Richard E. Bennett. *Choice* 25 (July–August 1988): 347.

Review of *Timber and the Forest Service* by David A. Clary. *Nevada Historical Society Quarterly* 2 (Summer 1988): 130–31.

Review of *A Companion for the Television Series* by Dean L. May. *Sunstone* 12 (May 1988): 38–39.

Review of *David Matthew Kennedy: Banker, Statesman, Churchman* by Martin B. Hickman. *BYU Studies* 28 (Spring 1988): 110–12.

Review of *American Forestry: A History of National and Private Cooperation* by William G. Robbins. *Pacific Historical Review* 57 (November 1988): 494–95.

Review of *The Forested Land: A History of Lumbering in Western Wash-

ington by Robert E. Ficken. *Western Historical Quarterly* 20 (February 1989): 74–75.

Review of *The Far West and the Great Plains in Transition, 1859–1900* by Rodman W. Paul, with editorial assistance of Martin Ridge. *Reviews in American History* 17 (March 1989): 85–89.

Review of *Water in New Mexico: A History of Its Management and Use* by Ira G. Clark. *Pacific Historical Review* 58 (February 1989): 126–27.

Review of *Zion in the Courts: A Legal History of The Church of Jesus Christ of Latter-day Saints, 1830–1900* by Edwin Brown Firmage and Richard Collin Mangrum. *BYU Studies* 29 (Summer 1989): 124–27.

Review of *Wildlife and the Public Interest: Nonprofit Organizations and Federal Wildlife Policy* by James A. Tober. *Choice* 27 (September 1989): 543.

Review of *The Twentieth Century West: Historical Interpretations* edited by Gerald D. Nash and Richard W. Etulain. *Utah Humanities News* (Spring 1990): 4.

Review of *Preserving Different Pasts: The American National Monuments* by Hal Rothman. *Utah Historical Quarterly* 58 (Spring 1990): 207–09.

Review of *The State of Deseret* by Dale L. Morgan. *Journal of the Southwest* 32 (Autumn 1990): 371–74.

Review of *America's Historic Landscapes: Community Power and the Preservation of Four National Historic Sites* by Ary J. Lamme. *Choice* 28 (September 1990): 617.

Review of *The American West: A Twentieth Century History* by Michael P. Malone and Richard W. Etulain. *Pacific Historical Review* 59 (November 1990): 572–73.

Review of *Wilderness Preservation and the Sagebrush Rebellions* by William L. Graf. *Choice* 29 (February 1991): 506.

with Rick J. Fish. Review of *Forest Service Photographs on Laser Video Disc. Agricultural History* 65 (Spring 1991): 188–89.

Review of *Challenge of the Big Trees: A Resource History of Sequoia and Kings Canyon National Parks* by Lary M. Dilsaver. *Choice* 29 (July–

August 1991): 548.

Review of *Splinters of a Nation: German Prisoners of War in Utah* by Allan Kent Powell. *American Historical Review* 96 (October 1991): 1322–23.

Review of *Reed Smoot: Apostle in Politics* by Milton R. Merrill. *John Whitmer Historical Association Journal* 11 (1991): 100–02.

Review of *Church, State, and Politics: The Diaries of John Henry Smith* edited by Jean Bickmore White. *Dialogue* 25 (Spring 1992): 171–73.

Review of *Lives of the Saints in Southeast Idaho: An Introduction to Mormon Pioneer Life Story Writing* by Susan Hendricks Swetnam. *Choice* 30 (July–August 1992): 612.

Review of *Mormon Polygamy: A History. 2nd ed.* by Richard S. Van Wagoner. *BYU Studies* 32 (Winter–Spring 1991): 295–98.

Review of *"It's Your Misfortune and None of My Own": A New History of the American West* by Richard White. *Utah Historical Quarterly* 60 (Fall 1992): 377–79.

Review of *Camp Floyd and the Mormons: The Utah War* by Donald R. Moorman. *Choice* 31 (February 1993): 531.

Review of *Victims: The LDS Church and the Mark Hofmann Case* by Richard E. Turley. *Choice* 31 (February 1993): 542.

Review of *Utes: The Mountain People* by Jan Pettit. *Journal of the West* 32 (January 1993): 97–98.

Review of *Mormons and Cowboys, Moonshiners and Klansmen: Federal Law Enforcement in the South and West* by Stephen Creswell. *Pacific Historical Review* 62 (February 1993): 96–97.

Review of *A Naturalist in Indian Territory: The Journals of S. W. Woodhouse, 1849–50* by S. W. Woodhouse. *Choice* 31 (July–August 1993): 569.

Review of *Trails: Toward a New Western History* by Patricia Nelson Limerick, Clyde A. Milner II, and Charles E. Rankin. *Pacific Historical Review* 62 (May 1993): 233–35.

Review of *The Unsolicited Chronicler: An Account of the Gunnison Massacre, its Causes and Consequences, Utah Territory, 1847–1859* by Robert Kent Fielding. *Choice* 31 (September 1993): 609.

Review of *A Mixed--but Generally Open--Bag: The Historical Articles in the Encyclopedia of Mormonism*. *Sunstone* 16 (November 1993): 39-42.

Review of *To Reclaim a Divided West: Water, Law, and Public Policy, 1848-1902* by Donald J. Pisani. *Pacific Historical Review* 62 (November 1993): 498-500.

Review of *Centennial West: Essays on the Northern Tier States* edited by William L. Lang. *Pacific Northwest Quarterly* 84 (October 1993): 154.

Review of *The Mormons' War on Poverty: A History of LDS Welfare, 1830-1990* by Garth L. Mangum and Bruce D. Blumell. *BYU Studies* 33 (1993): 785-90.

Review of *Dam that River!: Ecology and Mormon Settlement in the Little Colorado River Basin* by William S. Abruzzi. *Choice* 32 (February 1994): 461-62.

Review of *Utah Remembers World War II* by Allan Kent Powell. *Montana: The Magazine of Western History* 44 (Spring 1994): 92.

Review of *History of Idaho* by Leonard J. Arrington. *Choice* 32 (November 1994): 570.

Review of *Solemn Covenant: The Mormon Polygamous Passage* by B. Carmon Hardy. *Idaho Yesterdays* 38 (Fall 1994): 29-30.

Review of *Utah People in the Nevada Desert: Homestead and Community on a Twentieth-Century Farmers' Frontier* by Marshall E. Bowen. *Choice* 32 (February 1995): 540-41.

Review of *Senator Alan Bible and the Politics of the New West* by Gary E. Elliott. *Choice* 32 (June 1995).

Review of *The National Forests of the Northern Region: Living Legacy* by Robert D. Baker, Larry Burt, Robert S. Maxwell, Victor H. Treat, and Henry C. Dethloff, and *Centennial Mini-Histories of the Forest Service* by Terry L. West. *Public Historian* 17 (Spring 1995): 68-71.

Review of *Caring for Creation: An Ecumenical Approach to the Environmental Crisis* by Max Oelschlaeger. *Environmental History Review* 19 (Summer 1995): 89-91.

Review of *"At the Extremity of Civilization": A Meticulously Descriptive Diary of an Illinois Physician's Journey . . . to the Goldmines and

Cholera of California by Israel Shipman Pelton Lord, edited by Necia Dixon Liles. *Choice* 33 (September 1995).

Review of *Conspiracy of Optimism: Management of the National Forests since World War Two* by Paul W. Hirt. *Isis* 86 (December 1995): 690-91.

Review of *Cultures in Conflict: A Documentary History of the Mormon War in Illinois* by John E. Hallwas and Roger D. Launius. *Choice* 33 (March 1996): 4112.

Review of *Power from on High: The Development of Mormon Priesthood* by Gregory A. Prince. *Journal of American History* 83 (June 1996): 202-3.

Review of *Waters of Zion: The Politics of Water in Utah* by Daniel C. McCool. *Pacific Historical Review* 65 (November 1996): 686-87.

Review of *The Story of Big Bend National Park* by John Jameson. *Choice* 34 (January 1997).

Review of *Kingdom on the Mississippi Revisited: Nauvoo in Mormon History* edited by Roger D. Launius and John E. Hallwas. *Western Historical Quarterly* 28 (Spring 1997): 83-84.

Review of *Nineteenth Century Mormon Architecture and City Planning* by C. Mark Hamilton. *Church History* 66 (June 1997): 393-95.

Review of *Missing Stories: An Oral History of Ethnic and Minority Groups in Utah* by Leslie G. Kelen and Eileen Hallet Stone. *Choice* 34 (June 1997).

Review of *Mormons in Transition* by Leslie Reynolds. *Dialogue: A Journal of Mormon Thought* 30 (Fall 1977): 183-85.

Review of *The Mormon Hierarchy: Extensions of Power* by D. Michael Quinn. *Sunstone* 20 (December 1997): 65-67.

Review of *Necessary Fraud: Progressive Reform and Utah Coal* by Nancy J. Taniguchi. *Pacific Historical Review* 66 (November 1997): 608-09.

Review of *The Culture of Wilderness: Agriculture as Colonization in the American West* by Frieda Knobloch. *American Historical Review* 103 (April 1998): 606-7.

Review of *Desert Between the Mountains: Mormons, Miners, Padres, Mountain Men, and the Opening of the Great Basin, 1772-1869* by

Michael S. Durham. *Choice* 35 (March 1998): 4044.

Review of *The Lion of the Lord: Essays on the Life and Service of Brigham Young* edited by Susan Easton Black and Larry C. Porter. *BYU Studies* 37 (1997–98): 231–36.

Review of *Wyoming's Big Horn Basin to 1901: A Late Frontier* by Lawrence M. Woods. *Choice* 36 (September 1998): 539.

Review of *Friendly Fire: The ACLU in Utah* by Linda Sillitoe. *Pacific Historical Review* 67 (Fall 1998): 299–300.

Review of *Early Mormon Documents. Vol. 1* edited by Dan Vogel. *Church History* 67 (September 1998): 603–4.

Review of *Alexander William Doniphan: Portrait of a Missouri Moderate* by Roger D. Launius. *Military History of the West* 28 (Fall 1998): 227–28.

Review of *Glen Canyon and the San Juan Country* by Gary Topping. *Journal of American History* 85 (December 1998): 1095–96.

Review of *Charter for Statehood: The Story of Utah's State Constitution* by Jean Bickmore White. *Journal of Mormon History* 24 (Fall 1998): 226–30.

Review of *The History of Louisa Barnes Pratt: Being the Autobiography of a Mormon Missionary Widow and Pioneer* edited by S. George Ellsworth. *Choice* 36 (May 1999): 5276.

Review of *Mormon Midwife: The 1846–1888 Diaries of Patty Bartlett Sessions* edited by Donna Toland Smart. *Journal of the West* 38 (July 1999): 95.

Review of *Utah's Black Hawk War* by John Alton Peterson. *Choice* 36 (July/August 1999): 6484.

Review of *Forgotten Kingdom: The Mormon Theocracy in the American West, 1847–1896* by David L. Bigler. *New Mexico Historical Review* 74 (October 1999): 420–21.

Review of *Rainbow Bridge: An Illustrated History* by Hank Hassell. *Choice* 37 (March 2000): 4082.

Review of *Adventures of a Church Historian* by Leonard J. Arrington. *Journal of American History* 87 (June 2000): 312–13.

Review of *The Trial of Don Pedro Leon Lujan: The Attack Against Indian Slavery and the Mexican Traders in Utah* by Sondra Jones. *Choice* 37

(June 2000): 5859.

Review of *The Fish and Wildlife Job on the National Forests: A Century of Game and Fish Conservation, Habitat Protection, and Ecosystem Management* by Theodore Catton and Lisa Mighetto. *Environmental History* 5 (April 2000): 274–75.

Review of *As a Thief in the Night: The Mormon Quest for Millennial Deliverance* by Dan Erickson. *Journal of the West* 39 (Summer 2000): 107–8.

Review of *George Q. Cannon: A Biography* by Davis Bitton. *Utah Historical Quarterly* 68 (Fall 2000): 351–52.

Review of *Early Mormon Documents, Vol. 2* edited by Dan Vogel. *Journal of Mormon History* 26 (Fall 2000): 348–52.

Review of *The Lord's University: Freedom and Authority at BYU* by Bryan Waterman and Brian Kagel. *Journal of the West* 40 (Winter 2001): 113.

Review of *Nixon and the Environment* by J. Brooks Flippen. *Choice* 38 (June 2001): 5762.

Review of *Sojourner in the Promised Land: Forty Years Among the Mormons* by Jan Shipps. *Choice* 39 (September 2001): 262.

Review of *Irrigated Eden: The Making of an Agricultural Landscape in the American West* by Mark Fiege. *Journal of Mormon History* 27 (Fall 2001): 260–62.

Review of *Fawn McKay Brodie: A Biographer's Life* by Newell G. Bringhurst. *Nevada Historical Society Quarterly* 44 (Fall 2001): 295–97.

Review of *A Trial Furnace: Southern Utah's Iron Mission* by Morris A. Shirts and Kathryn H. Shirts. *Choice* 39 (February 2002): 3585.

Review of *Indian Reserved Water Rights: The Winters Doctrine in Its Social and Legal Context, 1882–1930s* by John Shurts. *Western Legal History* 13 (Summer/Fall, 2001): 268–70.

Review of *Hispanics in the Mormon Zion* by Jorge Iber. *Journal of Arizona History* 43 (Summer 2002): 192–93.

Review of *Army of Israel: Mormon Battalion Narratives*, edited by David L. Bigler and Will Bagley. *Montana: The Magazine of Western History* 52 (Summer 2002): 76–77.

Review of *The Great Thirst: Californians and Water: A History, Revised*

Edition by Norris Hundley, Jr. *Environmental History* 7 (July 2002): 515–16.

Review of *More Wives than One: Transformation of the Mormon Marriage System, 1840–1910* by Kathryn M. Daynes. *Journal of Mormon History* 28 (Fall 2002): 187–90.

Review of *Blood of the Prophets: Brigham Young and the Massacre at Mountain Meadows* by Will Bagley. *BYU Studies* 42, no. 1 (2003): 167–74.

Review of *Mormon History* by Ronald W. Walker, David J. Whittaker, and James B. Allen with a contribution by Armand L. Mauss. *Historian* 65 (Fall 2003): 1205–06.

Review of *Water and American Government: The Reclamation Bureau, National Policy, and the West, 1902–1935* by Donald J. Pisani. *Agricultural History* 78 (Winter 2004): 120–21.

Review of *American Massacre: The Tragedy at Mountain Meadows, September 1857* by Sally Denton. *Choice* 41 (February 2004): 3626.

Review of *All Abraham's Children: Changing Mormon Conceptions of Race and Lineage* by Armand L. Mauss. *Utah Historical Quarterly* 72 (Spring 2004): 177–79.

Review of *The Politics of American Religious Identity: The Seating of Senator Reed Smoot, Mormon Apostle* by Kathleen Flake. *Journal of Mormon History* 31 (Spring 2005): 181–84.

Review of *Joseph Smith: Rough Rolling Stone* by Richard L. Bushman. *Mormon Historical Studies* 6 (Fall 2005): 255–59.

Review of *The Politics of American Religious Identity: The Seating of Senator Reed Smoot* by Kathleen Flake. *Choice* 42 (2005).

Review of *Fort Limhi: The Mormon Adventure in Oregon Territory, 1855–1858, Kingdom in the West (vol. 6)* by David L. Bigler. *Oregon Historical Quarterly* 105 (June 2004): 327–28.

Review of *Joseph Smith* by Robert V. Remini. *Journal of Mormon History* 30 (Spring 2004): 219–221.

Review of *The Mormon Question: Polygamy and Constitutional Conflict in Nineteenth-Century America* by Sarah Barringer Gordon. *Nova Religio: The Journal of Alternative and Emergent Religions* 9 (August 2005): 119–21.

Review of *Brigham Young's Homes* by Colleen Whitley. *Nevada Historical Society Quarterly* 49 (Summer 2006): 155–57.

Review of *The Journals of a Forest Service Chief* by Jack Ward Thomas, edited by Harold K. Steen. *Environmental History* 10 (January 2005): 127–28.

Review of *Earth Repair* by Marcus Hall. *American Historical Review* 111 (October 2006): 1146–47.

Review of *Doing the Works of Abraham, Mormon Polygamy, Its Origins, Practice, and Decline,* volume 9 of *Kingdom in the West: The Mormons and the American Frontier,* edited by B. Carmon Hardy. *Journal of Mormon History* 34 (Summer 2008): 191–96.

Review of *The Lumberman's Frontier: Three Centuries of Land Use, Society and Change in America's Forest* by Thomas Cox. *Oregon Historical Quarterly* 112 (Spring 2011): 125–26.

Review of *Nauvoo Polygamy: We Called It Celestial Marriage* by George D. Smith. *BYU Studies* 50 (Summer 2011): 177–82.

Review of *In Heaven as it Is on Earth: Joseph Smith and the Early Mormon Conquest of Death* by Samuel Matthew Brown. *Choice* 49 (2012).

Review of *Parley P. Pratt, the Apostle Paul of Mormonism* by Terryl L. Givens and Matthew J. Grow. *Utah Historical Quarterly* 80 (Summer 2012): 276–77.

Review of *Fire Management in the American West: Forest Politics and the Rise of Megafires* by Mark Hudson. *Oregon Historical Quarterly* 113 (Winter 2012): 600–1.

Review of *Brigham Young: Pioneer Prophet* by John G. Turner. *BYU Studies* 52 (2013): 155–58.

Review of *Revelation, Resistance, and Mormon Polygamy: The Introduction and Implementation of the Principle* by Merina Smith. *Choice* 49 (January 2014).

Review of *A Foreign Kingdom: Mormons and Polygamy in American Political Culture, 1852–1890* by Christine Talbot. *Choice* 49 (July 2014).

Review of *Robert Newton Baskin and the Making of Modern Utah* by John Gary Maxwell. *Utah Historical Quarterly* 82 (Summer 2014):

236–37.

Review of *Roads in the Wilderness* by Jedediah Rogers. *Choice* 49 (May 2014).

Review of *Modern Polygamy in the United States: Historical, Cultural, and Legal Issues* by Cardell K. Jacobson and Lara Burton. *Choice* 49 (December 2014).

Review of *Remembering Iosepa: History, Place, and Religion in the American West* by Matthew Kester. *Western Historical Quarterly* 45 (Spring 2014): 67.

Review of *The Oxford Handbook of Mormonism* edited by Terryl L. Givens and Philip L. Barlow. *Choice* 53 (March 2016).

Review of *From the Outside Looking In: Essays on Mormon History, Theology, and Culture* edited by Reid L. Neilson and Matthew J. Grow. *Choice* 53 (June 2016).

Review of *Unpopular Sovereignty: Mormons and the Federal Management of Early Utah Territory* by Brent M. Rogers. *Montana: The Magazine of Western History* 67 (Summer 2017): 85–87.

Review of *Defender: The Life of Daniel H. Wells* by Quentin Wells. *Choice* 54 (May 2017).

Review of *A House Full of Females, Plural Marriage and Women's Rights in Early Mormonism, 1835–1870* by Laurel Thatcher Ulrich. *Choice* 55 (April 2018).

Review of *Sister Saints: Mormon Women Since the End of Polygamy* by Colleen McDannel. *Choice* 56 (May 2019).

Review of *The Next Mormons: How Millennials are Changing the LDS Church* by Jana Riess. *Choice* 57 (February 2020).

Review of *Pioneers in the Attic: Place and Memory Along the Mormon Trail* by Sara M. Patterson. *Choice* 58 (August 2021).

Review of *The Saints and the State: The Mormon Troubles in Illinois* by James Simeone. *Choice* 59 (May 2022).

Review of *Joseph Smith for President: The Prophet, the Assassins, and the Fight for American Religious Freedom* by Spencer W. McBride. *Choice* 59 (July 2022).

Review of *D. Michael Quinn: Mormon Historian* by Gary D. Topping. *Journal of Mormon History* 49 (January 2023): 131–33.

Review of *Brigham Young, Colonizer of the West: Diaries and Office Journals, 1832–1871*, edited by George D. Smith. *Journal of Mormon History* 49 (January 2023): 142–46.

Review of *Mormon Envoy: The Diplomatic Legacy of Dr. John Milton Bernhisel* by Bruce W. Worthen. *Journal of Mormon History* 49 (October 2023): 151–55.

Review of *Imperial Zions: Religion, Race, and Family in the American West and the Pacific* by Amanda Hendrix-Komoto. *Choice* 61 (January 2024).

Review of *Vengeance is Mine: The Mountain Meadows Massacre and its Aftermath* by Richard E. Turley Jr. and Barbara Jones. *Choice* 61 (February 2024).

Review of *Vengeance is Mine: The Mountain Meadows Massacre and its Aftermath* by Richard E. Turley Jr. and Barbara Jones. *Journal of Mormon History* 50 (February 2024): 149–52.

Review of *Joseph Smith's Gold Plates: A Cultural History* by Richard L. Bushman. *Choice* 61 (April 2024).

Review of *Dale L. Morgan: Mormon and Western Histories in Transition* by Richard L. Saunders. *Choice* 61 (2024).

Research Reports

"In the Shadow of the Brickman: Interstate Brick Company and Its Predecessor, 1891–1975." Prepared for the Interstate Brick Company. July 1975.

"Serving the Intermountain Construction Industry: The Development of Interstate Brick Company, 1891–1975." Prepared for the Interstate Brick Company. August 1975.

"Research and Interpretation of the Domingues–Escalante Trail Covering the Dates, September 25 to October 13, 1776." Prepared for the Federal–State Bicentennial Committee with Ted J. Warner. 1975.

"The Union Pacific Land Grant, Legislative Intent, and the Acquisition of Mineral Rights: A Case Study of the Formation and Implementation of Public Policy." Prepared for Anschutz Corporation. June 1980.

"The 1874 Settlers Relief Act and the Union Pacific." Prepared for

Anschutz Corporation. July 1980.

"The History and Development of the Mountain Dell Area: Including the Identification and Location of the Mormon Trail." With Charles E. Hughes, Stanley B. Kimball, and Marian A. Johnson. 1992.

"Ogden Arsenal, HAER UT–84." With Mary Troutman, Tom Carter, and others. Historic American Engineering Report completed for the National Park Service, Rocky Mountain Regional Office, and the Utah State Historical Society. 1996)

"Hill Field, HAER UT–85." With Mary Troutman, Tom Carter, and others. Historic American Engineering Report completed for the National Park Service, Rocky Mountain Regional Office, and the Utah State Historical Society. 1996.

"Report on Utah Apex Operations." Prepared for Arnold and Porter. January 28, 1997.

"The Pittman Silver Purchase Act." Prepared for Arnold and Porter. February 1997.

"Ore Mined from Utah–Apex." Prepared for Arnold and Porter. February 1997.

"Ore Mined, Shipped and Milled from Utah–Apex Properties, Following the Opening of the Bingham Creek Tailings Pond, 1914–1931." Prepared for Arnold and Porter. January 1997.

"Total Ore Mined and Purchase, Ore Milled, and Concentrates Recovered at the Mill and Tailings Deposited in Bingham Creek Tailings Pond by Utah–Apex Company, 1914–1931." Prepared for Arnold and Porter. January 28, 1997.

"Estimates of Total Ore Mined and Milled, Concentrates Recovered at the Mill, and Tailings Disposed of by Utah–Apex Mining Company, 1907–1913." Prepared for Arnold and Porter. February 17, 1997.

"Estimate of Tailings Deposited in Bingham Canyon and Creek by Utah Copper Company, 1904–1931." Prepared for Arnold and Porter. April 8, 1997.

"Estimate of Tailings Deposited in Bingham Canyon and Creek by Red Wing, Butler Liberal, North–Utah Mining, and associated Companies, 1900–1931." Prepared for Arnold and Porter. April 15, 1997.

"Estimate of Tailings Deposited in Bingham Canyon and Creek by Ohio Copper Company, Largely from the Winnamuck Mill, 1900–1931." Prepared for Arnold and Porter. May 5, 1997.

"Total Output of Lead and Estimate of Tailings Deposited in Bingham Creek by Ohio Copper Company Largely from the Winnamuck Mill, 1865–1899." Prepared for Arnold and Porter. May 5, 1997.

"Estimate of Tailings Deposited in Bingham Canyon and Creek by Lead Mine Mill, 1900–1931." Prepared for Arnold and Porter. May 5, 1997.

"Total Output of Lead and Estimate of Tailings Deposited in Bingham Canyon and creek by Lead Mine Mill, 1865–1899." Prepared for Arnold and Porter. May 5, 1997

"Estimate of Total Ore Mined, Total Ore Shipped Directly to the Smelters, and Total Ore Treated at Concentrating Mills, and Tailings in the West Mountain (Bingham) District, 1900–1915." Prepared for Arnold and Porter. May 6, 1997.

"Total Output of Lead and Estimate of Tailings deposited in Bingham Canyon and creek by Red Wing, Butler Liberal, North–Utah, and Associated Companies, 1865–1899." Prepared for Arnold and Porter. May 6, 1997.

"Estimate of Total Ore Mined, Total Ore Shipped Directly to the Smelters, Total Ore Treated at Concentrating Mills, and Tailings, in West Mountain (Bingham) District, 1916–1931." Prepared for Arnold and Porter. May 6, 1997.

"Estimate of Ore Mined and Milled, Concentrates recovered, and Tailings Generated by Bingham–New Haven (1904–1914) and Utah Metal & Tunnel (1915–1931) in the Bingham District." Prepared for Arnold and Porter. September 23, 1997.

"Estimate of Ore Milled, Concentrates Recovered, and Tailings Generated by the Wall Mill in Bingham Canyon, 1905–1931." Prepared for Arnold and Porter. September 1997.

"List of Mills Operating in the Bingham District, 1898–1933." Prepared for Arnold and Porter. October 23, 1997.

"Overview of the Development of Milling Operations in Bingham Canyon, 1974–1930." Prepared for Arnold and Porter. November

1997.

Declaration in *ACLU, et al. v. Salt Lake City and the Corporation of the Presiding Bishop*. January 13, 2004.

Critique of Sara Dant's expert witness report and testimony on the navigability of the Weber River at Peoa in Utah District Court, Salt Lake City. For Kirton–McConkie. 2014–15.

"Expert Opinion and Report of Thomas G. Alexander, Ph.D., on Traditional and Historic Public Access to Utah Waters for Fishing and other Non–Consumptive Activities." *Utah Stream Access Coalition v. VR Acquisitions, LLC, and State of Utah*, No. 1000500558. (Fourth District Court, Wasatch County). Submitted on behalf of Utah Stream Access Coalition, appellee and cross appellant. 2020.

Papers Presented

"Utah's Rise to the Precipice: The Economy, 1910–1920." Presented at the Utah State Historical Society Annual Meeting, Salt Lake City, UT, September 17, 1965.

Comment on "Irrigation Technology." Presented at the Western History Association Annual Meeting, El Paso, TX, October 15, 1966.

"Idaho Governor Mason Brayman: A Reconsideration." Presented at the Western History Association Annual Meeting, Tucson, AZ, October 18, 1968.

"John Wesley Powell, the Irrigation Survey, and the Inauguration of the Second Phase of Irrigation Development in Utah." Presented at the Utah State Historical Society Annual Meeting, Logan, UT, September 21, 1968.

Comment on "Trains, Workers and Unions--the Beginnings and Government and Railroads." Presented at the Golden Spike Symposium, Salt Lake City, UT, May 6, 1969.

Comment on "Bureaucracy and Reform in the West and the Indian Agent as Bureaucrat Some Alternative Views." Presented at the Organization of American Historians Annual Meeting, Los Angeles, CA, April 16, 1970.

"A Conservative Senator and Conservation, Reed Smoot and the Development of Public Land Policy, 1905–1920." Presented at the American Historical Association–Pacific Coast Branch Annual

Meeting, Portland, OR, September 4, 1970.

"The Federal Land Survey System and the Mountain West, 1870–1896." Presented at the History of the Territories, sponsored by the National Archives. Washington, DC, November 3, 1969.

"The Church and the Welfare State: An Historian's View." Presented at the Brigham Young University College of Social Sciences Faculty Forum. Provo, UT, April 29, 1970.

"The Price of Patriotism: Utah and the Depression of the Early 1920s." Presented at the American Historical Association–Pacific Coast Branch Annual Meeting, Santa Barbara, CA, CA, August 25, 1972.

"Reflections on the Sources for Reclamation History." Presented at the Fifth Annual Archives Administration Symposium, Salt Lake City, UT, November 11, 1972.

Moderator of the "Mormonism in the 20th Century" panel. Presented at the Utah Valley Chapter of the Utah State Historical Society, Provo, UT, February 1, 1973.

"The Depression of 1921 in Utah." Presented at the Brigham Young University Economics Department Seminar. Provo, UT, March 14, 1974.

"Reed Smoot and Conservation in the 1920s: Teapot Dome Revisited." Presented at the Brigham Young University Symposium on the Life and Political Thought of Reed Smoot. Provo, UT, March 19, 1974.

"Nauvoo History and the LDS and RLDS. Churches Today." Presented at the Mormon History Association Annual Meeting, Nauvoo, IL, April 21, 1974.

"Ideology and the Development of Environmental Policy." Presented at the Brigham Young University Symposium on Environmental Law and Policy. Provo, UT, April 23, 1974.

"Wilford Woodruff and the Changing Nature of Mormon Religious Experience." Presidential Address presented at the at the Mormon History Association Annual Meeting, April 12, 1975.

Comment on "The Mormons and Economic Thought." Presented at the Brigham Young University Department of Economics "Economics and the Mormon Culture" symposium, Provo, UT, October 6, 1975

"The Utah Legislature and the New Political History, 191-1917: A Multiple Regression Analysis." Presented at the Western History Association Annual Meeting, Tulsa, OK, October 11, 1975.

Comment on "'The Testimony of the Covenant,': The Spiritual Dimension of the Kirtland Experience." Presented at the Mormon History Association Annual Meeting, Kirtland, OH, April 23, 1977.

"The Place of Joseph Smith in the Development of American Religion: A Historiographical Inquiry." Presented at the Mormon History Association Annual Meeting, Logan, UT, May 5, 1978.

"Ogden: A Federal Colony in Utah." Presented at the Utah State Historical Society Annual Meeting, Ogden, UT, September 16, 1978.

"Second Reconstruction: the LDS Church and the Utah Politics in the 1920's." Presented at a meeting sponsored by the Utah State Historical Society and the Utah Endowment for the Humanities, March 8, 1979.

"The LDS Church and the Social Gospel: The Social Advisory Committee as a Case Study." Presented at the Mormon History Association Annual Meeting, Lamoni, IA, May 26, 1979.

"Collegiality in the Council of the Twelve." Presented at The Church of Jesus Christ of Latter-day Saints Historical Department, Salt Lake City, UT, August 21, 1979.

"To Maintain Harmony: Collegiality and the Council of the Twelve." Presented at the American Historical Association Annual Meeting, New York, December 28, 1979.

"The Reconstruction of Mormon Doctrine: From Joseph Smith to Progressive Theology." Presented at the Mormon History Association Annual Meeting, Canandaigua, NY, May 3, 1980.

"From Principle to Commandment: The Adoption of the Current Interpretation of the Word of Wisdom, 1898-1933." Presented at the Second Annual Sunstone Theological Symposium, Salt Lake City, UT, August 22, 1980.

Comment on "Persistences that Differ" by Paul Edwards. Presented at the Second Annual Sunstone Theological Symposium, Salt Lake City, UT, August 23, 1980.

"The Union Pacific Land Grant, Legislative Intent, and the Acquisition of Mineral Rights." Presented at the Potomac Westerners. Washington, DC, February 25, 1981.

"Utah War Industry During World War II: A Human Impact Analysis." Presented at the Utah Centennial Foundation's Military History Symposium, Salt Lake City, UT, August 15, 1981.

"'That He will Yet Reveal': An Approach to the Theology of Joseph Smith." Presented at the Indiana University Religious Studies Department and Lilly Foundation Seminar on Joseph Smith and Mormonism, December 4–5, 1981.

"A New and Everlasting Covenant." Presented at the Sunstone Theological Symposium, Salt Lake City, UT, August 38, 1982.

Comment on "Early Twentieth Century Political History." Presented at the Mormon History Association Annual Meeting, May 8, 1982.

"Water Resources and Community Values: Utah's Dixie as a Case Study." Presented at the Washington County Historical Society–Utah Endowment for the Humanities lecture series. Hurricane and St. George, UT, March 23 and 24, 1983.

"World War II in Ogden and Utah." Presented at the Ogden Kiwanis Club, Ogden, UT, April 6, 1983.

Comment on "Mid-Twentieth Century Mormon Leaders." Presented at the Mormon History Association Annual Meeting, Omaha, NE, May 7, 1983.

Panelist in a panel discussion on the subject: "The Intellectual in the Service of the Faith." Sunstone Theological Symposium, Salt Lake City, UT, August 26, 1983.

"Salt Lake City in the Progressive Era: A Comparative Perspective on Voluntary Organization in Western Cities." Presented at the Western History Association Annual Meeting, October 13, 1983.

Comment on "Interpreting the Mormon Past." Presented at the Mormon History Association Annual Meeting, Provo, UT, May 10, 1984.

"Progress on the Regional History." Presented at the Supervisors and Regional Foresters Meeting, Ogden, UT, April 24, 1984.

"Public Resource Policy and the Forest Service in the Intermountain

West: The Struggle for Multiple Use." Presented at the Utah State Historical Society Annual Meeting, August 18, 1984.

Comment on "The Theological Influence of Bruce R. McConkie" by David John Buerger. Presented at the Sunstone Theological Symposium, August 25, 1984.

"Covenant Theology in the Teachings of Joseph Smith." Presented at the John Whitmer Historical Association at Graceland College, Lamoni, IA, May 1, 1985.

"Historical Methodology and the New Mormon History: One Historian's View." Presented at the Mormon History Association Annual Meeting, Independence, MO, May 4, 1985.

"Professionalization of Range Management in Region 4 of the US Forest Service, 1910–1929: The Caribou National Forest and the Great Basin Experiment Station as Models." Presented at the Western History Association Annual Meeting, Sacramento, CA, October 11, 1985.

Comment on "Literary Life in Early Utah." Presented at the Mormon History Association Annual Meeting, Salt Lake City, UT, May 3, 1986.

"The Forest Service and the LDS Church: Utah Forests as a Test Case." Presented at the Utah Valley Historical Society Meeting, February 11, 1986.

"The Livestock Industry and Forest Service Land Regulation." Presented to the rangers, forest supervisors, and regional officials of the Intermountain Region, Boise, ID, March 18, 1986.

Comment on "An Adventurer and a Missionary: Two Mid–Nineteenth Century Mormons in the Sandwich Islands." Presented at the American Historical Association–Pacific Coast Branch Annual Meeting, Honolulu, HI, August 14, 1986.

"Reflection on the History of Region 4." Presented at the Intermountain Region Old Timers Club. Ogden, UT, August 19, 1986.

"Die Europäische Missionen, 1900–1930: Die Schweirigkeiten vom Verbreiten des Evangeliums in frühen Zwansigten Jahrhundert." Presented at the HLT Forum symposium on LDS History and Culture, Kassel, West Germany, August 30, 1986.

"The Forest Service and the LDS Church in the Mid-Twentieth Century: Utah National Forests as a Test Case." Presented at the Weber State College Dello G. Dayton Memorial Lecture, Ogden, UT, April 15, 1987.

"Timber Management and Environmental Deterioration: The Case of the Intermountain Region, 1950-1985." Presented at Duke University to the Forest History Society-American Society for Environmental History Conference on Forests, Habitats, and Resources, Durham, NC, May 2, 1987.

Comment on "American Social History." Presented at the Weber State College Utah Academy of Sciences, Arts, and Letters Annual Meeting, Ogden, UT, May 8, 1987.

"Men, Women, Families, and Vocation in the Mid-nineteenth Century: The Lives of Wilford and Phebe Woodruff, 1844-1846 as a Case Study." Presented at the Mormon History Association Annual Meeting, Oxford, England, July 6, 1987.

Comment on "Mormons on the Underground." Presented at the Pacific Coast Branch--American Historical Association Annual Meeting, Los Angeles, CA, August 18, 1987.

"The Relationship of Water Resources to Other Resources in The American West." Presented at the Western History Association Annual Meeting, Los Angeles, CA, October 10, 1987.

"Wilford Woodruff and the World of the Early Nineteenth Century Religious Seeker." Presented at the Mormon History Association Annual Meeting, Logan, UT, May 7, 1988.

Comment on "Cattle Ranching, the Powell Expedition, and Western Writers." Presented at the Utah Academy of Sciences, Arts, and Letters Meeting, St. George, UT, May 13, 1988.

"Pillars of my Faith: New Testament Christianity and the Book of Mormon." Presented at the Sunstone Symposium, Salt Lake City, UT, August 19, 1988.

Comment on "Wood and Water in the Northwest: Development and Controversy." Presented at the Western History Association Annual Meeting, Wichita, KS, October 13, 1988.

"The Federal Constitution and Government in the Western Territories:

Theory and Practice in Ruling America's Transcontinental Empire." Presented at a lecture series commemorating the bicentennial of the American constitution, Anchorage, AK, January 27, 1989.

Comment on "Fawn M. Brodie, 'Mormonism's Lost Generation,' and No Man Knows My History" by Newell G. Bringhurst and "Dale Morgan, the Writer's Project, and Mormon History as a Regional Study" by Charles S. Peterson. Presented at the Mormon History Association Annual Meeting, Quincy, IL, 13 May 1989.

"The American Religious Context." Presented in the Brigham Young University symposium "At Nauvoo: The City of Joseph, 1839–1989," Provo, UT, September 21, 1989.

"The Historical Background of Water-Use Policy in Utah." Presented at the Environomics Symposium, Park City, UT, September 22, 1989.

"Wilford Woodruff, Intellectual Progress, and the Growth of an Amateur Scientific and Technological Tradition in Early Territorial Utah." Presented at the American Historical Association–Pacific Coast Branch Meeting, Tacoma, WA, August 14, 1989.

"Writing Histories for Utah's Centennial" with Ronald W. Walker. Presented at the Western History Association Annual Meeting, Tacoma, WA, October 14, 1989.

Comment on "Historical Perspectives on the Mormon Church." Presented at the Society for the Scientific Study of Religion Annual Meeting, Salt Lake City, UT, October 28, 1989.

"The Manifesto as a Watershed Event in Utah History: Reflections on the Impact of Wilford Woodruff's Manifesto on the People of Utah." Statehood Day Address presented in St. George, UT, January 4, 1990. Presented again to the meeting of the Utah Valley Branch of the Utah State Historical Society. Provo, UT, October 9, 1990.

"The Odyssey of a Latter-day Prophet: Wilford Woodruff and the Manifesto of 1890." Presented at the Mormon History Association Annual Meeting, Laie, HI, June 14, 1990.

"Reclamation and the Strawberry Valley Project." Presented to the Strawberry Valley Water Users Association. Payson, UT, July 11,

1990.

"Introduction to Rural Communities." Presented at the Symposium on Rural Villages in the Twenty-first Century, Logan, UT, July 20, 1990.

"Intellectual Change and Wilford Woodruff's Manifesto." Panel discussion presented at the *Sunstone* Symposium, August 24, 1990.

Comment on "A Twentieth Century Mormon Conflict: Polygamy and the 'Fundamentalists.'" Presented at the Western History Association Annual Conference, Reno, NV, October 19, 1990.

"Mormon Polygamy." Presented at a seminar on Utah History at Utah Valley Community College, Orem, UT, March 20, 1991.

Comment on "The Hauns Mill Massacre and Dissent in Missouri." Presented at a symposium on the LDS Church in Missouri, March 29, 1991.

"Wilford Woodruff and the Mormon Reformation of 1856–1857." Presented at the Mormon History Association Annual Meeting, Claremont, CA, May 31, 1991.

"Mormon Primitivism and Modernization." Presented at a conference titled "Christian Primitivism and Modernization: Coming to Terms with Our Age," Malibu, CA, Pepperdine University, June 8, 1991.

"Putting the Text into Context." Presented at a Utah State University conference on writing biography and family history, Logan, UT, June 25, 1991.

"The Gilded Age and the Progressive Era." Presented at an Advanced Placement American History Institute, Golden West College, Huntington Beach, CA, June 27, 1991.

"Experiences of a Young Boy in World War II." Presented at a Brigham Young University conference on Utah in World War II. Provo, UT, June 28, 1991.

"Salt Lake City During the Progressive Era: A Western City Meets Twentieth-Century Challenges." Presented as the Phi Alpha Theta Luncheon Address, Western History Association Annual Meeting, October 17, 1991.

"The Sources for Forest Service History in the Denver, Seattle, and San

Bruno Branches of the National Archives" and "Preparing Forest Service History for Publication." Presented at the Symposium on Forest Service History, Salt Lake City, UT, January 30, 1992.

"Critique of Janet Fishburn's 'The Presbyterian Sexuality Report, A Case Study in the Languages of Moral Discourse.'" Presented at the Indiana University Purdue University at Indianapolis Symposium on Public Discourse and Religion, Indianapolis, IN, April 4, 1992.

"The Education and Growth of a Mormon Prophet--Wilford Woodruff." Presented to the Miller-Eccles Study Group, Arcadia, CA, April 18, 1992.

"The LDS Church and the Wasatch Oasis Environment: Stewardship, Reverence, and Exploitation, 1847-1930." Presented at the Mormon History Association Annual Meeting, St. George, UT, May 16, 1992.

"Some Suggestions on Writing Biography: The Case of Wilford Woodruff." Keynote Address presented at the Evans Biography Workshop "Biography is High Adventure." Logan, UT, June 22, 1992.

Comment on "Changing Values, Policy Reform, and Techno-fixes in Post World War Two National Forest Management." Presented at the American Society for Environmental History Conference, Pittsburgh, PA, March 4, 1993.

"Historical Perspectives on Hydroelectric Power in Utah." Presented at the Future of Western Energy Conference, Park City, UT, April 1, 1993.

"Mormon History for the Near Future." Presented at the Mormon History Association Annual Meeting, Lamoni, IA, May 21, 1993.

Comment on "Change, Change, and More Change." Presented at the Western History Association Annual Meeting, Tulsa, OK, October 14, 1993.

"Academic Freedom and Committed Scholarship Revisited: The Challenge to a Church-owned University." Presented at the American Society for Church History American Historical Association Annual Meeting, January 8, 1994.

"Cooperation, Conflict, and Compromise: Women, Men, and the Environment in Salt Lake City, 1890-1930." Presented for the

Brigham Young University Karl G. Maeser Distinguished Faculty Lecture. Provo, UT, February 16, 1994.

"An Apostle in Exile: Wilford Woodruff and the St. George Connection." Presented for the Juanita Brooks Lecture, St. George, UT, February 1994.

"The Ambivalence of the New Mormon History." Presented at the Mormon History Association Annual Conference, Park City, UT, May 20, 1994.

"The LDS Church and the Environmental Movement in Salt Lake City, 1890–1930." Presented to the Miller–Eccles Study Group, Arcadia, CA, June 12, 1994.

"Utah's Constitution: A Reflection of the Territorial Experience." Presented at a symposium honoring the centennial of Utah's constitution, Salt Lake City, UT, May 8, 1995.

"Sylvester Q. Cannon and the Revival of Environmental Consciousness in the Mormon Community." Presented at the Mormon History Association Annual Meeting, Kingston, Canada, June 24, 1995.

"The Meanings of Utah's History." Presented at the Utah State Historical Society Annual Meeting, Salt Lake City, UT, July 13, 1995.

"Salt Lake City: City Beautiful, City Functional, or City Polluted." Presented at the Western History Association Annual Meeting, Denver, CO, October 14, 1995.

"Utah's Constitution: A Reflection on the Territorial Experience." Presented at the Utah State Historical Society symposium "Celebrate the Centennial," January 3, 1996.

"The Great Depression, World War II, and the Transformation of Utah from a Colony of Wall Street to a Colony of Washington." Presented at the Brigham Young University eleventh annual Russel B. Swensen Lecture. Provo, UT, March 14, 1996.

"The Utah State Constitution and Community Reconciliation." Presented at the Brigham Young University Utah Centennial Symposium, Provo, UT, April 20, 1996.

Comment and critique of "Mormon Intellectual History: A Prospectus for the Future." Presented at the Mormon History Association Annual Meeting, Snowbird, UT, May 17, 1996.

Comment and critique of "Race, Gender, and Ethnicity within Mormonism." Presented at the American Historical Association–Pacific Coast Branch Annual Meeting, San Francisco, CA, August 9, 1996.

"Lowell Bennion's Theology and Its Importance in Mormon Theology." Presented at the Sunstone Symposium, Salt Lake City, UT, August 15, 1996.

"The Limits of LDS Power in Utah Since Statehood." Presented at the banquet session of the Regional Pi Sigma Alpha Meeting, Salt Lake City, UT, March 19, 1997.

"Joseph Smith, Brigham Young, Parley P. Pratt and Mormon Environmental Theology as an Aspect of the Creation, Sin, the Fall, Redemption, the Gathering, Zion, and the Millennium." Presented at the Mormon History Association Annual Meeting, Omaha, NE, May 24, 1997.

"A Meaning for the Latter-day Saint Westward Movement." Presented at a panel discussion on Mormon culture. University of Munich, Germany, June 18, 1997.

"Reflections on the Meaning of the Latter-day Saint Past." Presented at the University of Halle, Halle, Germany, June 9, 1996. Presented in a revised form to LDS Institute students at Hannover (June 11), Berlin (June 12), and Heidelberg (June 14); to seminary students at Nürnberg (June 21); and to a fireside in Nürnberg (June 15) and Munich (June 22).

"Building Zion, Restoring, Eden, and Preparing for the Millennium: Nineteenth Century Mormon Prophets and the Environment." Presented at the American Historical Association–Pacific Coast Branch Annual Meeting, Portland, OR, August 10, 1997.

"Wilford Woodruff and His Families." Presented at the Miller–Eccles Study Group, Arcadia, CA, April 18, 1998.

Comment on "Mormons and the American Context: Church–State Relationships." Presented at the Mormon History Association Annual Meeting, Washington, DC, May 23, 1998.

"Utah's Transformation from Kingdom to Colony, to Commonwealth." Presented to the Wasatch Front Economic Council, September 23,

1998.

Chair of session entitled "Polygamy as a Social Phenomenon: Academic Perspectives." Presented at the Utah Valley State College Symposium on Plural Marriage, Orem, UT, November 16, 1998.

"The Great Depression and the Change the Structure of Utah's Economy." Presented at the History Lecture Series of the Utah State Historical Society and Utah State Archives, Salt Lake City, UT, March 18, 1999.

"A Provo Native and Environmentalism in the Early Twentieth Century: The Case of Reed Smoot." Presented at the Provo Golden Kiwanis. Provo, UT, April 5, 1999.

"Struggle in an Endangered Empire: The Search for Total Ecosystem Management in the Forests of Southern Utah, 1976–1997." Presented at the American Society of Environmental History Annual Conference, April 15, 1999.

"Wilford Woodruff and Zion's Camp: Baptism by Fire and the Spiritual Confirmation of a Future Mormon Leader." Presented at the Mormon History Association Annual Conference, May 21, 1999.

"The Future of Mormon Historical Studies." Presented at the Mormon History Association Annual Conference, May 22, 1999.

"Public Policy and the American West." Presented at the *Journal of Policy History* Annual Conference, May 28, 1999.

"Inevitable Conflict: Recreation and Commodity Use in the Forests of the Intermountain Region." Presented at the American Historical Association–Pacific Coast Branch Annual Conference," Maui, HI, August 7, 1999.

"Reed Smoot as an Environmentalist." Presented at the Provo Sesquicentennial Conference, Provo, UT, Brigham Young University, September 10, 1999.

"William McLellin and the Independent Restorationist Tendency in Early Mormonism." Presented at the Western History Association Annual Conference, Portland, OR, October 7, 1999.

"Mormon Communitarianism in Utah." Presented at Alta High School, Sandy, UT, November 16, 1999.

"Joseph Smith, Parley P. Pratt, Brigham Young and Nineteenth Century Mormon Environmental Theology." Presented at the Brigham Young University Eco-Response, Provo, UT, February 29, 2000.

"Mormons and the Environment." Presented at the University of Colorado Symposium on Nature and Religion, March 10, 2000.

"Comparison of Mormonism and Radical Environmentalism." Presented at the Conference on Spiritual Frontiers, March 31, 2000.

Comment on "Telescopes and Tornados: Western Climate and International Science." Presented at the Western History Association Annual Conference, San Antonio, TX, October 13, 2000.

"Reed Smoot and Conservation in the West." Presented at the Utah Westerners, Salt Lake City, UT, October 17, 2000.

"The Development of a Pastoral Landscape in Utah's Wasatch Oasis." Presented in a series on Utah's pastoral landscapes at the Brigham Young Univeristy Museum of Art. Provo, UT, February 9, 2001.

"Irrigating the Mormon Heartland: The Operation of the Irrigation Companies in Wasatch Oasis Communities, 1847–1880." Presented at the Mormon History Association Annual Conference, May 19, 2001.

"Mutual Irrigation Companies in Utah, 1847–1880." Presented at a University of Nevada, Reno, conference on Water and Rural Life Reno, NV, June 2, 2001.

Chair and commentator at the Phi Alpha Theta Session. Presented at the Western History Association Annual Meeting, San Diego, CA, October 7, 2001.

"Putting Your Chapter Forward." Participant in panel discussion at the Phi Alpha Theta Biennial Convention, San Antonio, TX, December 28, 2001.

"Utah's Wasatch Front and the Development of a Pastoral Landscape." Presented at the Utah Valley State College Symposium on Landscape and Art, Orem, UT, March 6, 2002.

"Mormon Prophets, Urban Gathering, and Care for God's Creations: Cases from the Nineteenth Century." Presented at the American Society for Environmental History Annual Meeting, Denver, CO, March 22, 2002.

"Watering the Mormon Heartland: Irrigation Companies and Modernization in Utah's Wasatch Oasis, 1870-1930." Presented at the Bureau of Reclamation Symposium, Las Vegas, NV, June 18, 2002.

Chair of session "Crossing Borders: Different Perspectives." Presented at the American Historical Association–Pacific Coast Branch Annual Meeting, Tucson, AZ, August 2, 2002.

"Red Rock and Grey Stone: Reed Smoot, the Establishment of Zion and Bryce Canyon National Parks, and the Rebuilding of Downtown Washington, D.C." Presidential Address presented at the American Historical Association–Pacific Coast Branch Annual Meeting, Tucson, AZ, August 3, 2002.

"Amazing Advocate: Senator Reed Smoot's Role in Establishing National Parks." Presented at the Weber State Univeristy Utah Construction/Utah International Symposium, Ogden, UT, October 10, 2002. Presented again for the Brigham Young University—Hawaii Department of History, Laie, HI, August 7, 2003.

Chair of session "Mormons and African Americans." Presented at the Western History Association Annual Convention, Colorado Springs, CO, October 18, 2002.

"Wilford Woodruff and the Nauvoo Experience." Presented at the Ninth Annual Utah Pioneer Symposium Sponsored by the Sons of Utah Pioneers, Salt Lake City, UT, October 26, 2002. Presented again at the Senior Missionary meeting, Laie, HI, August 4, 2003.

Comment on "The Brigham City Cooperative." Presented at the Mormon History Association Annual Conference, Painesville, OH, May 24, 2003.

"The Stake President as Progressive Entrepreneur, Edward H. Snow and the St. George Stake." Presented at the Edward H. Snow Family Organization Meeting, St. George, UT, June 13, 2003.

"Interdependence and Change: Mutual Irrigation Companies in Utah's Wasatch Oasis in an Age of Modernization, 1870–1930." Presented at the Pacific Coast Branch–American Historical Association Annual Meeting, Honolulu, HI, August 1, 2003.

Chair and Commentator at the Phi Alpha Theta Session of the Pacific Coast Branch–American Historical Association Annual Meeting, Honolulu, HI, August 2, 2003.

Chair, session on "Mormon Polygamy." Presented at the Western History Association Annual Meeting, Fort Worth, TX, October 10, 2003.

"Salt Lake City during the Progressive Era." Presented at the Utah Westerners, October 21, 2003.

"Reed Smoot and the Establishment of Zion and Bryce National Parks." Presented at the Utah Valley Historical Society Meeting, November 11, 2003.

Chair and commentator on "United States Social History." Presented at the Phi Alpha Theta Biennial Conference," New Orleans, LA, January 17, 2004.

"Mormon Prophets and the Environment: Creation, Sin, the Fall, Redemption, and the Millennium." Presented at a symposium entitled Sacred Stewardship: LDS Perspectives on Nature, Provo, UT, February 28, 2004.

"Church and Community: Latter-day Saint Women in the Progressive Era, 1890–1930." Presented at the New Scholarship on Latter-day Saint Women in the Twentieth Century Symposium, Provo, UT, March 20, 2004.

Chair of session "Memory, Perception and Environmental Regulation." Presented at the American Society for Environmental History Annual Meeting, Victoria, British Columbia, Canada, April 3, 2004.

Chair of and commentator in session "Images of Mormon Women." Presented at the Mormon History Association Conference, Provo, UT, May 22, 2004.

"Assessing an Argument about the Significance of the Reed Smoot Hearings as Mormonism Made Its Way into the Twentieth Century." Presented at the Mormon History Association Conference, Provo, UT, May 22, 2004.

"Considering Matters of the Spirit in Biography." Presented at the Evans Biography Conference, Utah State University, Logan, UT, June 11, 2004.

Comment on "The Mountain Meadows Massacre." Presented at the Mormon History Association Conference, Caspar, WY, May 26, 2006.

"Brigham Young, the Quorum of the Twelve, and the Latter-day Saint Investigation of the Mountain Meadows Massacre." Presented as the Leonard J. Arrington Lecture, Logan, UT, September 21, 2006.

"Carpetbaggers, Reprobates, and Liars: Federal Judges and the Utah War." Presented at the Mormon History Association Conference, Salt Lake City, UT, May 25, 2007.

"The Odyssey of a Mormon Prophet: Wilford Woodruff and the Manifesto." Presented at the symposium "Wilford Woodruff: Missionary, Apostle, and Church President," Provo, UT, October 12, 2007.

"David Eccles and the Origins of Utah Construction Company–Utah International." Presented at the Utah International Symposium, October 18, 2007.

"Carpetbaggers, Reprobates, and Liars: Federal Judges and the Utah War (1857–58)." Presidential Address presented at the Phi Alpha Theta Annual Convention, Tamaya Resort, NM, January 4, 2008.

"Latter-day Saints and Violence in the Nineteenth Century." Presented at the Western History Association Annual Meeting, Salt Lake City, UT, October 24, 2008.

"Thomas L. Kane and the Mormon Problem in National Politics." Presented at the In Honorable Remembrance, Thomas L. Kane and the Latter-day Saints Lecture Series, December 10, 2008.

"Mission to Danger: Edward Hunter Snow and the Southern States Mission, 1886–1888." Presented at the Mormon History Association Annual Convention, Springfield, IL, May 22, 2009.

"Church Administration in the Progressive Era." Presented at the Brigham Young Univeristy Church History Symposium, February 26, 2010.

"Critique of Matthew Grow, . . . *Thomas L. Kane* . . ." Presented at the *BYU Studies* Symposium, Provo, UT, March 13, 2010.

"Reed Smoot and the Founding of Zion National Park." Presented at the meeting of the Utah Valley Historical Society, Provo, UT, May 11, 2010.

"The Stake President as Family Man, Edward Hunter and Hannah Nelson Snow and their Family." Presented at the annual conference of the Mormon History Association, Kansas City, MO, May 28, 2010.

"Utah's Constitution: Origins, Development, Revisions." Presented at the meeting of the Utah State Historical Society, Utah State Capitol Building, September 9, 2010.

"Conflict, Fraud, and Inaction: The Administration of Public Lands in Territorial Utah." Presented at the annual conference of the Western History Association, Lake Tahoe, NV, October 14, 2010.

"Edward Hunter Snow and the Founding of Southern Utah University (1897) and the Founding and Operation of Dixie College (1907–1932)." Presented at the annual conference of the Mormon History Association, St. George, UT, May 28, 2011.

"Political Partisanship in Twentieth Century Utah." Presented at a Brigham Young University symposium on political partisanship, Provo, UT January 24, 2012.

Comment on "Straddling the Border." Presented at the Mormon History Association Annual Conference, Calgary, Alberta, Canada, June 30, 2012.

Comment on "Denver C. Snuffer's *The Consolidation of Church and State: Brigham Young's Telestial Kingdom*." Presented at the Sunstone Symposium, Salt Lake City, UT, July 28, 2012.

"Carpetbaggers, Reprobates, and Liars: Federal Judges and the Utah War." Presented at the Conference of the American Association for State and Local History Ninth Circuit Court and US Supreme Court Luncheon, October 5, 2012.

"Stake President Edward Hunter Snow and the Modernization of Utah's Dixie." Presented at the St. George Tabernacle, UT, October 19, 2012.

"Lost Memory and Environmentalism: Mormons in Utah, 1847–1930." Presented at the Brigham Young University symposium on the Environment in the West, Provo, UT, November 2015.

Comment on "James B. Allen's *Still the Right Place*." Presented at the Utah State Historical Society's Annual State History Conference, West Valley City, UT, October 11, 2017.

Comment on "Thomas Simpson's *American Universities and the Birth of Modern Mormonism, 1867–1940*." Presented at the Mormon History Association Annual Convention, St. Louis, MO, June 2,

2017.

Comment on "Kenneth L. Cannon's 'The Surprising Relationship of James E. Talmage, PhD, and James E. Homans, PhD, (aka Robert C. Webb).'" Presented at the Mormon History Association Annual Convention, St. Louis, June 2, 2017.

Comment on "Mormon Settlement in San Berndardino." Presented at the Mormon History Association Conference, May 2018.

Comment on "'The Evils of a Dole Abolished': The Church Welfare Plan and Mormon Visions of Self Sufficiency." Presented at the Mormon History Association Conference, June 2019.

Moderator in session titled "Author Meets Critics: Gordon Shepherd and Gary Shepherd, *Jan Shipps, A Social and Intellectual Portrait: How a Girl from Hueytown, Alabama, Became a Renowned Mormon Studies Scholar.*" Presented at the Mormon History Association Conference, June 2019.

Presenter in a session on his biography of Brigham Young. Presented at the Mormon History Association Conference, Park City, UT, 2021.

Response to speakers in a session on the body of his work. Presented at the Western History Association, Portland, OR, 2021.

Participant and speaker in a session on the organization of the Mormon History Association, Presented at the Mormon History Association Conference, Logan, UT, June 2022.

Chair and Commentator for Christian Scientists in Zion. Presented at the Mormon History Association Conference, Rochester, NY, June 2023.

"The Odyssey of a Latter-day Prophet: Wilford Woodruff and the Manifesto of 1890." Presented at the Wilford Woodruff Association Meeting, West Valley City, UT, February 3, 2024.

Consultation

National Endowment for the Humanities, 1976, 1978, 1979, 1980, 1981, 1982, 1983, 1984, 1985, 1986, 1988, 1995, 2003.

Consultant on the Escalante–Domingues Trail in Utah, National Geographic Society, 1977.

The Anschutz Corporation; Martin, Pringle, Schell & Fair; and Clyde

and Pratt on federal railroad land policy, 1978–1985.
Commission on the Federal Impact Aid Program, 1980.
University of Nebraska Press, 1980.
DC Heath and Co., 1980, 1990.
University of Nevada Press, 1980, 1987, 2000.
University of Utah Press, 1981, 1986, 1987, 1988, 1989, 1995, 2004, 2006, 2015, 2016.
Consultant on the Central Rocky Mountain area, National Geographic Society, 1984.
Consultation with Vatican Secretariat Monseigneur Lajola on the History of Mormonism in the Far West, September 22, 1985.
Consultation and interview on modern Mormonism with Bobby Berleffi, PBS, October 20, 1985.
Color commentary with Randall Carlisle and Michelle King on funeral of President Spencer W. Kimball, Channel 2, Salt Lake City, UT, November 9, 1985.
Signature Books, 1985, 1987, 1988.
University of Illinois Press, 1985, 1986, 1987, 1988, 1989, 1990, 1991, 1992, 1993, 1994, 1995, 1996, 1997, 1999, 2001, 2002, 2003, 2009.
Consultation and television interview with Maria Taylor on environmental problems in Wyoming for a documentary by Focus Productions, PBS, May 9, 1986.
Interview with Jerry Pond on the history of Salt Lake City, Voice of America, June 12, 1986.
Consultation on Utah and Mormonism, Voice of America, 1986, 1987.
Consultation on the "Utah" entry, *World Book Encyclopedia*, 1986, 1995.
Consultation on the history of Region 2 (the Rocky Mountain Region) with Wayne Hinton, Forest Service, 1986–88.
Member of Core Group of Consultants for the Project on Religion and American Culture, Indiana–University–Purdue University at Indianapolis, 1986–1990.
Outside reviewer for the evaluation of their program, Center for Colorado Plateau Studies, Northern Arizona University, April 18, 1988.
University of Oklahoma Press, 1988, 1991, 1993, 1998, 2003, 2015,

2016, 2017.

Consultant on the history of Utah, Smithsonian Institution, August 1988.

Ezra Taft Benson Food and Agriculture Institute, 1989.

Utah State University Press, 1989, 1991, 1993, 1994, 1997, 1998.

Consultation and interview with Roger Hansen on the history of the Strawberry Valley Reclamation Project, Bureau of Reclamation, 1989–90. This resulted in part of a television program.

Consultant on the Transcontinental Railroad, Peace River Films, 1990.

Consultant on the Mormon Trail from Nauvoo to Salt Lake Valley, National Park Service, 1990.

Interview on Mormon History and the Practice of Polygamy, KUED–TV, January 8, 1990.

John Prince Show, K–TALK (KTKK) Radio, January 9, 1990.

Interview on Polygamy and the Manifesto, K–TALK (KTKK) Radio, September 26, 1990.

Interview on Utah during the Civil War, K–TALK (KTKK) Radio, September 28, 1990.

Journal of Forest and Conservation History, 1991, 1995.

"Isis: An International Review Devoted to the History of Science and its Cultural Influences," 1992.

Interview with Kevin Stanfield on the role of The Church of Jesus Christ of Latter-day Saints in Utah politics, KKAT Radio, January 22, 1992.

Consultation on research in the National Archives Branches and publishing forest history, Forest Service, January 30, 1992.

Television interview on the role of John Wesley Powell on the development of irrigation in the West, Palo Alto, CA, March 11, 1992.

Consultation and a televised interview on John Wesley Powell and Irrigation in the West, Bureau of Reclamation, Palo Alto, CA, March 11, 1992. This resulted in a video on Powell.

Interview and consultation on the history of Mormonism, Arts and Entertainment Channel, November 1992. This resulted in part of a television program in Spring 1993.

Agricultural History, 1994.

Interview and program on Latter-day Saints and life choices, VISN, the Interfaith Satellite Network (Notre Dame University), 1994.
Pacific Historical Review, 1994, 1996.
Principle historical consultant and interviewee for a program on Utah history for the centennial of Statehood, KUED–TV, 1994–95.
Consultant on the Secondary Education Social Studies Core Curriculum Revision, Utah State Government, June 1995.
Interview with Philip Adams for a program on Latter-day Saints, Australian Broadcasting Company, December 11, 1995.
Consultation and referee for manuscripts, *Western Historical Quarterly*, 1995, 2001
Consultant n Hill Air Force Base and Ogden Arsenal, National Park Service, 1995–1996.
"The Achievement of Statehood as Reconciliation." BYU Emeritus Alumni Association, January 15, 1996.
Talk and radio broadcast on *Utah, The Right Place*, University of Utah, January 18, 1996
Talk to Friends of University of Utah Library, University of Utah, January 21, 1996.
Luncheon Speaker at Conference Sponsored by Data Center, Utah State Government, University Park Hotel, January 25, 1996.
Interview on Van Hale's Religion on the Air program, K–TALK (KTKK) Radio, January 28, 1996.
Seminar for advanced placement teachers on the Progressive Era, Jordan School District, February 1, 1997.
Interview with Amanda Pollak on the Scofield Coal Mine Disaster, David Gruben Productions, May 13, 1997.
Videotaped interview with Molly Ryan for a program on the Mormons for PBS, FilmRoos, July 16, 1997.
The Geographical Review, 1997.
Consultant for a Washington, DC, law firm on the history of mining in Bingham Canyon and mine tailings along Bingham Creek, Arnold and Porter, 1997–1998.
Interview with Victoria Slind–Flor, National Law Journal, 1998.
Religion and American Culture, 1998.
Interview for program on Mormonism in the Progressive Era, KUED–

TV, May 13, 1998.

Interview with Leslie Bennetts on Latter-day Saint Polygamy, *Vanity Fair*, November 1998.

Member of the PhD committee for David Pulsipher, University of Minnesota, 1998–99.

Interview with Sammy Linebaugh for a series of programs on Utah in the twentieth century, KTVX (Chanel 4), March 19, 1999.

Interview with Jenny Brundeen for a program on Mormons and the environment, KUER, April 13, 1999.

Interview with John Kowalewski on the history of Utah in the 20th century, *Ogden Standard Examiner*, May 1999.

Interview with Don Sider on communitarianism and polygamy in Utah, *People* magazine, May 1999.

Interview on current problems, KUER, June 1999.

Consultation on significant events and people in the 20th century, *Daily Herald*, Provo, UT, Fall 1999.

Interview with John Daley for a program on the inauguration of light rail in Salt Lake City, KSL, November 30, 1999.

Preparation of a list of ten prominent Utahns of the 20th century for Jay Shelledy, *Salt Lake Tribune*, December 1999, January 2000.

Consultant for a seven-state project on the Colorado River, Arizona Humanities Council, 1999–2002.

Referee, *Environmental History*, 2000.

The Journal of Interdisciplinary History, 2000.

Interview and panel discussion with Jim Bell on the history of the LDS Church, 1890–1920, and a discussion on the American presidency for a series on that subject, KBYU, March 17, 2000. Aired April 24, 2000.

Consultation about the Cathedral of the Madeleine, *Salt Lake Tribune*, July 2000.

"Trek West." Interview for a film on 19th-century Church of Jesus Christ of Latter-Day Saints Presidents, September 6, 2000.

Review of book manuscript, State University of New York Press, 2001.

University of New Mexico Press, 2001.

Interview with Larry Wright for a story on Mormonism, *The New Yorker* magazine, March 2, 2001.

Consultation and televised interview for a story on polygamy in Utah, NBC Dateline, May 2001.

Consultation for an article on the relationship between Mormons and their neighbors in Utah, *Salt Lake Tribune*, December 2001.

Consultant for an article manuscript, Nevada Historical Society, 2001–2002.

Televised interview on history of mining in Utah with Paul Gibram Begum, July 11, 2002.

Interview with Carma Wadley about the Colorado River, June 8, 2002. *Deseret News*, June 13, 2002.

Interview with Carole Makita for a story on Mormons and change in Utah, KSL, July 9, 2003.

Interview with Carrie Moore about Michael Leavitt, Mormons, and the Environment, August 13, 2003. *Deseret News*, August 16, 2003.

Interview with Jenifer K. Nii on State Street, *Deseret News*, November 6, 2003.

Interview on the role of The Church of Jesus Christ of Latter-day Saints in Utah, *Associated Press*, April 2003.

Interview with Howard Berkes for a story on John Wesley Powell, irrigation, and Latter-day Saints, NPR, July 23, 2003. Aired August 25, 2003.

Interview with David Sharp on the construction of dams and irrigation works by Latter-day Saints in the late 19th and early 20th centuries, *VIA* magazine, September 3, 2003.

Critique of a paper by Roy A. Prete for a publication on faithful history, November 2003.

External review of associate professor candidacy of James Whiteside, University of Colorado, 2003.

Arthur Clark Publishing Company, 2003–2004.

Church of Jesus Christ of Latter-day Saints, Presiding Bishop's Office, 2003–04.

Utah Museum of Art and History, National Advisory Council, 2003–2004.

Consultation on *ACLU et al. v. Salt Lake City and Corporation of the Presiding Bishop* for Alan Sullivan, January 2004.

Television interview for Temple Hill Videos for a program on the Salt Lake Temple with Lyman Dennis, March 17, 2004.

Interview with Nancy Green for a program on Utah and Mormon culture, KUED-TV, June 1, 2006.

Interview for Anderson Cooper 360 on Mormonism and Polygamy, CNN, May 10, 2006.

Interview with Jennifer Dobner on polygamy and The Church of Jesus Christ of Latter-day Saints, Associated Press, September 20, 2006.

Interview on polygamy, La Percera, Chile, October 2, 2006.

Interview with Marc Giauque for a story on the development of Downtown Salt Lake City, KSL, October 5, 2006.

Interview with Martin Stelv on the Salt Lake LDS Tabernacle, *The New York Times*, October 19, 2006.

Outside review for Kevin Fernland's advancement to professor, University of Missouri, 2011.

Numerous interviews with Glenn Rawson and Dennis Lyman for *History of the Saints* programs on KSL Channel 5, 2011–2014.

Interview with Guy Adams for the article "America's first Mormon President?" *The Independent*, May 2011.

Expert Witness on lawsuit on the Weber River, Kirton–McConkie, 2014–2015.

Expert witness for Orange Street in *Utah Stream Access Coalition v. Orange Street*, Kirton–McConkie, 2015.

Expert witness for Coburn, Peterson, Young, and Battle for Utah Stream Access Coalition, *Utah Stream Access Coalition v. VR Acquisitions*, 2019–2020.

"Christian Scientists in Zion" podcast recording, September 25, 2023.

Community Service

Voting District Chair, Democratic Party, 1972–73.

Neighborhood Chairman, Indian Hills District, Provo, City, 1993–94.

Provo City Landmarks Commission, Member, 1994–present; Vice Chair, 1995–96; Chair, 1996–1999.

Utah Capitol Art Placement Subcommittee, 2001–2004.

Works in Progress

History of the interaction of people and the environment in the Wasatch region (untitled)
Personal autobiography (untitled)

Teaching Experience
American History Survey, including Honors Section
Emergence of Modern America, 1865–1920
Western History
Historical Methodology (History 490)
American Culture, 1865–1914 (American Studies)
American Heritage (Interdisciplinary survey of Historical, Political and Economic aspects of United State development)
Sources and Problems in US History, 1865–1920
Sources and Problems in Western History
Utah History (History 364)
Sources and Problems in Mormon History
History of the Church of Jesus Christ of Latter-day Saints, to 1844
History of the Church of Jesus Christ of Latter-day Saints, since 1844
Junior Tutorial
United States Economic History
Sources and Problems in 20th Century United States History
Sources and Problems in Utah History
The Work of the Historian (History 200)
American Environmental History (History 394)

Service in The Church of Jesus Christ of Latter-day Saints
Stake Missionary, Ben Lomond Stake, 1952–1956.
Missionary, West German Mission, January 1956 to August 1958.
Sunday School Teacher, Ogden 29th Ward, 1958–59.
Sunday School Teacher, Utah State University 5th Ward, 1959–60.
Teacher's Quorum Advisor, Lafayette–Orinda Ward, 1960–61.
Activity Counselor in the YMMIA, Lafayette–Orinda Ward, 1961–62.
Early Morning Seminary Teacher, Lafayette–Orinda Ward, 1961–62.
Activity Counselor in the YMMIA, Lafayette–Orinda Ward, 1963–64.
Master M–Man, 1964.
Assistant Ward Clerk, Edgemont 3rd Ward, 1964–65.

Elder's Quorum President, Edgemont 3rd Ward, 1965.
Second Counselor in the Bishopric, Edgemont 3rd Ward, 1965–68.
High Priests' Group Leader, Edgemont 3rd Ward, 1968–70.
Instructor in the Melchizedek Priesthood Group, Carbondale Branch, 1970–71.
Sunday School Teacher, Carbondale Branch, 1971.
Ward Finance Committee Chairman, Edgemont 3rd Ward, 1971–72.
High Priests' Group Leader, Edgemont 3rd Ward, 1972–73.
Assistant Executive Secretary and Acting Executive Secretary, Edgemont Stake, 1973–78.
Stake High Councilman, Edgemont South Stake, 1978–82.
Gospel Doctrine Class Sunday School Teacher, Arlington, Va., Ward, 1981.
Bishop, BYU 133rd Ward, 1982–1986.
Priests Quorum and Explorer Advisor and Young Men's President, Edgemont 11th Ward, 1986–1988.
Gospel Doctrine Class Sunday School Teacher, Edgemont 11th Ward, 1988–1990.
Blazer B Class Teacher in Primary, 1991.
Chairman, Scout Troop Committee, Troop 769, Edgemont 11th Ward, 1991–92.
Ward Executive Secretary, Edgemont 11th Ward, 1992–1994.
Gospel Doctrine Class Sunday School Teacher, Edgemont 11th Ward, 1994–1995.
Second Counselor in the Bishopric, Edgemont 11th Ward, 1995–1996.
First Counselor in the Bishopric, Edgemont 11th Ward, 1996–2003.
Gospel Doctrine Class Sunday School Teacher, Edgemont 11th Ward, 2003–2004.
Missionary, CES Outreach Program, Berlin Germany, 2004–2005.
High Counselor, Berlin Stake, 2004–2005.
Missionary, LDS Church Family History and History Department, 2005.
Volunteer, LDS Church Family History and History Department, 2006.
Sunday School President, Edgemont 11th Ward, 2006–2007.
Second Assistant in the High Priests Group Leadership, Edgemont 11th Ward, 2007–2008.

First Assistant in the High Priests Group Leadership, Edgemont 11th Ward, 2008–2011.
Sunday School President, Edgemont 11th Ward, 2011–2013.
Gospel Doctrine Class Sunday School Teacher, Edgemont 11th Ward, 2013–2014.
Assistant Ward Clerk for Finance, Edgemont 11th Ward, 2014–2016.
Ward Historian, Edgemont 11th Ward, 2016–2023.
Instructor in High Priests Group, Edgemont 11th Ward, 2016–18.
Gospel Doctrine Sunday School Teacher, Edgemont 11th Ward, 2020–2023.
First Counselor in the Elder's Quorum Presidency, Edgemonth 11th Ward, 2023–present.

www.ingramcontent.com/pod-product-compliance
Lightning Source LLC
Chambersburg PA
CBHW070433010526
44118CB00014B/2020